BANKS OF THE TAMASA

A Story of Sita

by

VANDANA NITTOOR

Dear Anne,

I hope you enjoy reading my book!

With love

Vandana

This book is dedicated to my dear friend, guide and mentor
Dr. Dan Gottlieb

The painting on the front cover of this book is a reproduction of a 16th century fresco in the Veerabadra Temple in the village of Lepakshi in South India.

This beautiful temple dates back to the Vijayanagara Empire that thrived in South India between the 14th and 17th centuries CE. Lepakshi is my ancestral village and this temple has been a source of inspiration for me as long as I can remember.

The original frescoes have been damaged by water and the elements over the centuries. In this painting, I have attempted to fill these in to the best of my ability. I have used watercolors and have also attempted to adhere to the color scheme and the prevalent drawing style of the period.

~ Vandana Nittoor

Published by Bluebreath, LLC
PO Box 3 Voorhees, NJ, 08043

Cover Art: Vandana Nittoor
Cover & Book Design: Kena Design, Bangalore
(www.kenadesign.com)

ISBN: 978-0-692-46423-6

Printed by CreateSpace, An Amazon.com Company

CONTENTS

ACKNOWLEDGMENTS

Many people have been instrumental in influencing me to write this book—more than I can acknowledge here. So let me begin by apologizing to all my friends and family members whose special purpose in my life stands unacknowledged. I value the presence of each of you within my life!

People who have influenced my writing seem to have sprung into my life as randomly as a sneeze! The desire to hold on to you is entirely mine, as I try, greedily, to take another dip in the healing waters of company among kindred spirits.

Ed Claflin, who patiently suggested ways to infuse life into my sentences, has contributed generously towards my book as its editor. I could not have accomplished this difficult task without his help in understanding what I wanted to say. I sincerely appreciate all the support and encouragement that I received from him.

The design team at Kena Design has kindly contributed in designing and formatting this book. I thank them for their effort and generosity.

Badri Nittoor, my dear husband, my best friend and champion for my cause, put aside his own work and altered his busy schedule to help me complete this book. At the risk of antagonizing his overly sensitive wife, he suggested several corrections that were needed to make this book the living, breathing thing that it has become. This partnership of ours has enabled each of us to blossom and to find reassurance in each other's company, a place that we also call home. Indeed, Badri is my better half and I am proud to say so!

Esha and Maya, my beloved children, are my inspiration and my joy! Had it not been for these two young women, this book would have been published at least six months earlier. Yet, they are reason my heart beats and my blood flows, and I am forever in their debt for the riches they bring to my life.

Appa and Amma, my loving parents, encouraged and supported this endeavor, providing me with their blessing and approval. Even after all these years, I admit that I take great joy in making them proud of my simple accomplishments! I feel blessed and grateful.

Popeye, my faithful puppy, my soul mate and my son! Indeed there are days when I find strength to face the world only because I have complete faith in his undying love for me--love that is felt and expressed without restraint – in a manner that only puppies do! The warmth of his tiny body lying patiently upon my lap while I wrote this book will remain etched upon my heart and soul forever. We are truly fortunate to have him in our lives.

I thank you one and all!

×

INTRODUCTION

Across the world, and in all religions, there are stories of men who have left their homes in order to find their "true selves." The words of these men define a lifelong journey, undertaken to find lasting inner peace.

Women have accepted these precepts – spoken and written by men – but with awkwardness. Though similar in physique to their male counterparts, women are unique in psyche! How can we women find our true selves while remaining an integral part of the lives of those we deeply love and care about?

In this book I have sought to address the issue of women having to find a way to inner peace that aligns with our quintessential nature as nurturers and protectors of life.

This book does not profess bra-burning feminism, nor does it advocate imitating men in the name of equality and freedom. We are an angry lot – and justifiably so! But is this anger taking us any closer to happiness or wellbeing? Anger alienates us from men, who are our companions and compatriots. Activism and the imitation of male roles has brought attention and success to a few of our causes, but has also made us more misunderstood and harried. It has pushed us to pursue standards that are impossible to accomplish as we struggle to balance work and home.

In today's world too, crimes against women continue unabated. There remain places in the world where women are denied basic rights and privileges that men are entitled to. In pursuing our cause, we have carelessly forgotten to recruit the support of fathers, husbands, brothers, sons, and friends. Without the help and understanding of men, we cannot succeed.

But first, each of us needs to understand her own self, her inner needs, her compulsions and motivations.

This book is about finding our "self" as women in the thick bustle of caring, supporting and nurturing life all around. The story is about the return to our innermost essence without feeling the need to equate or measure up to men in every activity or arena.

This book is about giving permission to ourselves to just be whoever we truly are!

The character named Sita is central to the story I tell.

Why Sita?

In the timeless epic Ramayana, Sita is the consort of Rama and the epitome of perfection. She is portrayed as the "ideal" woman, self-sacrificing, caring, pious, faithful, modest, and obedient. The image of this woman as an ideal has become embedded in the psyche of the Indian people. Even modern-day India is not entirely free from the expectation that women should behave like the persona of Sita. The portrayal of her in the Ramayana confronts both men and women alike.

In that great epic, Sita lives a life that is mostly removed from joy and happiness. Married as a child to Prince Rama, she follows him to the kingdom of Ayodhya just as she is expected to do. When the prince's father, King Dasharatha, exiles Rama into the forest for a period of fourteen years, Sita devotedly follows her husband into the forest and makes a home of the shelter he builds for her. While living there, she is abducted by the demon Ravana and forced to live as captive in his kingdom of Lanka. When Rama finally reaches Lanka, a great battle ensues in which Rama kills Ravana and frees Sita from the demon's clutches. Prince Rama accepts his innocent wife only after her trial-by-fire in which she succeeds in proving her purity.

At the end of his fourteen-year exile, Rama returns from the forest, bringing Sita back to Ayodhya, and is crowned king. But Rama is unable to mitigate rumors questioning Sita's chastity arising from her captivity in Lanka. In an attempt to appease his citizens, Rama banishes a pregnant Sita to the forest. Abandoned and alone, a fear-filled Sita is given refuge by the kind Sage Valmiki. She gives birth to twin sons, Lava and Kusha, in his hermitage.

In the original account of the Ramayana written by the sage Valmiki, Sita's role is designated to be that of a passive follower. She is an obedient woman, a silent sufferer who accepts her lot in life in keeping with the rules of convention. Very little is said about her life and experience in the hermitage of sage Valmiki, where she lives until the end of her life. While she symbolizes strength and piety, she is no closer to finding peace within her life than are we modern-day women.

In the Ramayana, Sita's silent suffering and ageless sorrow make her seem dispirited and passive. It appears as if she does not live her own life but, rather, goes through life following the path established for her by men. They seem to enter and leave her life without their presence being sanctioned by her, one way or the other.

In this book I have employed my own imagination to describe the evolution that this woman underwent in the hermitage of Valmiki. I have forced Sita to scrutinize her own assumptions about life and embark on the sacred pilgrimage of self-realization.

As a woman, I too have struggled immensely with the many expectations that others have had of me; with my own expectations of myself; and with my insatiable spirit that has refused to mend its ways. I have been unable and unwilling to cower down when asked to, conform to convention, or allow myself to dissolve without expression into anonymity. I guess my resistance was an imperative. I finally succumbed to a breakdown that left me far more deeply depressed than I had been through much of my life.

As a result of the godly help, guidance, deep affection, and love that I received from Dr. Dan Gottlieb, not only did I recover but I was able to unearth those submerged parts of me that were drowned due to my own ignorance and assumptions about my life. The journey I have been on has been eye opening and life affirming. With greater knowledge I have been able to transform my deep anger into compassion. It has also earned me a great friend in Dan, who not only sat with me during my darkest hour but also entertained me with his rare sense of humor.

The many conversations we have had, and the many lessons I have learned from Dan, have helped shape this book. So many of my words resonate with the deep wisdom that he has imparted to me that I wish to dedicate this work of mine to him.

I sincerely hope this book will be of great help to anyone who reads it. Suffering – even great suffering – becomes tolerable when we see purpose within its many folds. Growth is painful, and inner growth is not free of deep scrutiny and forced examination of customs and values that we unconsciously hold on to. But freedom is neither true nor lasting if it is not from within.

   With this I seek to end my note and hope that you truly enjoy my work.

✕

I

CHASING GHOSTS

The roaring currents of the river Tamasa almost drowned the sounds of the men and horses hurrying along its banks. Shocked and stupefied, Sita's lower body with its pregnant belly lay motionless upon the soft grass even as she jolted her head and struggled to wake up. The crack of the whip against the hindquarters of the horses, the crunch of soil weighed down by the wheels of massive chariots, the rattle of bells tied to the gold-decorated parasol under which she had been riding, the loud cry of her brother-in-law Lakshmana demanding that the charioteers hurry up, the dust, the chaos, the senselessness, the unexplained betrayal – all that had happened within seconds – stunned her into silence.

"Forgive me, kind sister! I am only obeying my King's orders," Lakshmana yelled out as he drove away at great speed.

They had left! All of them! Each and every one! They had left, leaving her behind!

In instinctive haste Sita rose and ran towards the dust of the speeding chariots, forgetting the large belly that weighed heavily upon her soft feet. The dust faded and then disappeared altogether; her body grew wearier as sweat dripped down her long spine and soaked her clothes. Her breath echoed in the stillness of her strange surroundings while the hot, blazing summer sun, hovering in the blue cloudless sky, shone mercilessly upon her uncovered head. She gave up her chase and stopped abruptly, still pleading with the long-gone convoy of heartless men to come back for her.

The truth finally caught up with her, she was abandoned and all alone. They were never coming back for her. Her breath was heavy and her anxious eyes studied her surroundings in great panic.

The pre-dusk, dense forest stood motionless with not even a breeze to interrupt her hoarse cry. The piercing silence of the tall trees, the formless bushes interspersed among those trees like black smoke from a funeral pyre, the thick and tedious song of the indifferent crickets, the strangeness of the accidental pathways that seemed to invite fears from all directions, made her end seem real.

The wild beasts in the forest snarled and roared in the distance as her body trembled. Her sweaty palms clutched the ends of her embroidered sari, her eyes were filling up with tears as her throat attempted to heave out the liquid fear that swirled in her stomach. She felt the grime of the red soil rub in-between her toes, as she stood uncertain of the direction she should turn.

The fierce, flowing waters of the river seemed to dislike her fear-filled intrusion. All around her, the world stood like a placid, powerful witness too indifferent to intercede and prevent this abnormal cruelty.

Suddenly, she crumpled onto the earth in a heap and drenched it with her warm tears. Like a mop cloth, she had been discarded, left airless in a forgotten corner where she would forever leave her stain. Tears that mapped her soft cheeks flowed endlessly, dripping onto her chest, punctuated by loud gasps that resounded in her deaf surrounding. She, Queen Sita, had been ousted from the great city of Ayodhya unceremoniously like a wretched, worthless creature.

A fiery anger engulfed her as the full brutality of his cowardly act crawled into her, gnawing at her insides until they seemed to collapse. Her beloved Rama, the king of Ayodhya, who she imagined would never hurt her in any way possible, who had given her his sacred oath of protection, who had loved and cherished her as a dear husband – he had stealthily planned her betrayal. Compelled by rumors, and paying great heed to public opinion, he had conveniently set-aside his promises and disowned her in her greatest hour of need. She cursed the fate that linked her intimately to men who caused her unbearable suffering.

The heartbeat of the child in her swollen belly wanted to reassure her. Uncorrupted by the ways of the world and innocent to its functioning, it wanted to hold faith in life and its creator. But its voice was too soft to counter the wave of grief that had overcome the mother. The death that she suddenly wished for did not come, as she sat upon the ground dismayed at the uncertainty clouding her future and that of her unborn child.

But she had died! A silent, painful, invisible death – the kind that, without bothering to first snuffle out breath, kills from within, stealthily ridding the fragile sense of self, plucking at it leisurely one piece at a time – the death that does not wait, does not hesitate and does not discriminate. Queen Sita, wife to Rama the ruler of the world, daughter of mother Earth and the illustrious King Janaka, cherished daughter-in-law to the great King Dasharatha and his queens, loving sister to many, loyal friend and companion. – who was she chasing anyway? Who were these people she ran after, following behind chariots that were disappearing in the dust?

Ghosts!

Ghost of a husband who had sentenced her into exile! Ghosts of family that stood by and did nothing to stop him! Ghosts of citizens who pretended to love their queen! Ghosts of friends and servants who had vowed to be loyal! Ghosts of everyone she had ever known! They had all disappeared, dissolving like fog into the bright sun that scorched the earth and burnt her feet.

As the sun descended, the dark forest grew eerily silent, birds flew back home, the wind that had suddenly picked up rustled amongst the dry vines and leaves. The thick hum of indifferent crickets closed in and filled her with anguish.

Feeling frozen and incapable of moving from her spot, her tears resumed once again and she let out a shrill, echoing cry.

"So is this how it ends? Is this where I have come to die?" Sita asked aloud, in-between her loud sobs, addressing no one in particular.

But a soft voice spoke back.

"Cry!" he said.

"Cry all those tears that were stopped by temporary consolations. The tears that stopped as the breast was offered to you as an infant! The tears held back in the safe arms of your father who cared for you as a child! The tears that are unnoticed by the great King Rama! The tears that filled the eye but were held back in shame at the hands of the evil Ravana who abducted you! The tears that question your origin and purpose in life! The tears that speak of your aloneness in the world with no refuge or home to fall upon! The tears that plead for death hoping that it will be granted! Do not hold a single tear behind, for they all have to be emptied!"

"You have to be emptied! Emptied of your hopes, your dreams, your disappointments, your failures, your joys, your sources of joy and the self you have known. Perhaps then, if then you are still standing and you choose to embrace the emptiness before you, will you see! You will see that I never left and have been with you from the very beginning."

Sita glanced hesitatingly in the direction of the man who was speaking, but her eyes, filled with terror, were too afraid to look into his face; she glared at his dusty feet. His words were harsh but his voice was soft. Was she to be abducted again?

Her body quivered and shook as she remembered the strength of the arms that had grabbed her years before. She vividly recollected her helplessness, the shame, the deep, deep shame, the laughter, his crazed laughter that had filled her ears as she collapsed in his chariot. Was it happening once again?

Sita's breath felt too light and was leaving her, her head spun. Unable to sit up, she collapsed onto her side upon the earth.

Sage Valmiki stepped closer to Sita with his entourage of disciples. Sita's dust-covered face was marked by streams of tears, her rich clothing was crumpled and covered with grime, blisters had formed upon her burnt feet, her lips were dry and her pregnant belly rose against her helpless body. The kind sage teared up, his discomfort growing as he witnessed her plight.

He directed his disciples to carry Sita to his hermitage. The night sky loomed over them as they made their way back to his home. There, the women placed Sita gently upon a roughly sown mattress in one of the cluster of huts that traced the center of this tranquil dwelling.

The revered sage's hermitage was renowned for providing a refuge for the rejected, protection for the vulnerable, knowledge to all seekers, and compassion for those who were suffering. Thus, in incomprehensible haste, Sita had entered a new chapter in her life, and it patiently waited for her to come around and accept wholeheartedly the newness that had come with it!

✕

II

ANOTHER NEW BEGINNING

The golden rays of the early morning sun highlighted Valmiki's luminous, reddish-brown features. His smooth gray hair was neatly wound around his head, fixed in a hastily tied, odd-looking tuft at the top. A broad nose, delicate eyebrows and a long white flowing beard, distinguished his face. His garment of white cotton with red embroidered patterns on the edges was wrapped around him in folds, holding his aged but sturdy frame with a reverent grace.

Austere in his practice, he greeted this morning just as he had greeted all other mornings – with openness and surrender to its will. The previous day had been marred by the unforeseen events that had brought pregnant young Sita under his care; his heart felt soft with warm compassion at the plight of the expectant mother.

He did not understand the nature of laws that governed the world outside the hermitage, nor did he aspire for such understanding. As far as Valmiki was concerned, understanding the world with intellect alone was seriously limiting. While humans could pretend – like a snail trapped in a shell – that their own shell was the world, there were layers and universes far beyond the imagined vista that remained inaccessible to us.

He had, himself, chosen to live a more compassionate existence – showing tolerance for the inevitability of suffering that each of us causes and that each suffers in the hands of others. This was the founding principle of his hermitage. Everything within its territory was protected. Protection was granted to all denizens – the people, the trees, the plants, the birds that had nested in this territory, and the animals that might stray within.

Valmiki sat cross-legged, in silent meditation, under the huge banyan tree in the center of the hermitage. His eyes remained closed even when he heard small footsteps approach him; he smelled a whiff of jasmine as something was placed upon his head.

Then he heard a giggle, stifled as soon as it had begun, giving away the child playing this silly prank. Valmiki noticed the change in his internal landscape, a result of this silly intervention, and went back to his meditation unhindered.

When he finally opened his eyes – eyes that sparkled with a quivering aliveness – he saw a bunch of his youngest students sitting quietly before him. None was more than six years old. Seated on their straw mats, they looked clean in their cotton apparel, with neatly combed hair. Each of the boys wore a dhoti, which was a piece of cloth wrapped around their waist and legs, pleated in the front and folded gracefully at the small of the back. The girls wore long skirts with hand-printed blouses. Their hair was braided and decorated with fresh flowers. Along the periphery of the imagined borders of this open classroom, small wooden slippers were laid out in a straight line.

"Are you done, Guru?" asked Vasudeva, adding, "What did you pray for today?"

Valmiki heaved a long breath and replied, "I asked for small things in my prayer today. I asked for a gentle breeze under the hot sun, I asked for a hearty meal and some laughter, I asked that I not feel the need to prove, even to myself, the worthiness of my existence, and after a few other small things, I asked that perhaps I find absolute quiet and remain undisturbed while I meditate. Simple things, really!"

"And did you get all that you asked for?" questioned Tejas, an impetuous five-year-old whose eyes were filled with mischief.

Valmiki continued, "I'm not sure! It's a little like when you ask your mother to play with you when she's busy preparing dinner. She refuses, not because she is mean or dislikes you in any way, but just because its not... err.... convenient. She may just place a jasmine flower on your head instead! Am I right, Tejas?"

Saying so, he lifted the jasmine wreath that had been balanced on his own head and handed it over to the child.

The boy's face lit up brightly, and he smiled gorgeously as he offered his soft apology. "So, it is true, you can see us even when your eyes are closed. Mother was right!" he concluded with a look of awe.

It was Valmiki's turn to smile. With this, the lively brigade got busy with the day's lessons.

Not far away from all this spirited energy, Sita woke up in a sparsely furnished hut to find a woman draped elegantly in a sari sitting right by her, quietly separating cotton fluff from the seeds. Something about the woman's calm demeanor, the drifting sounds of children uttering their morning prayers, and the simplicity of her surrounding stirred absolutely no fear in Sita. Instead, she simply felt curious.

Noticing that she was awake, the woman smiled a bright smile and spoke in a soft, unhurried voice, "Welcome to the hermitage of Sage Valmiki, dear one! You are safe and protected out here. I have prepared some food and brought in some fresh water for you. The great sage has directed that I let him know when you are awake, and I must hurry to do so. Is there anything that I can do for you before I leave? I promise I will be back soon."

A bit bewildered at the turn of events, barely attentive to the woman's question, Sita nodded and whispered that she was all right.

It was not until the woman left that Sita slowly began to take in her surroundings. She was lying on a roughly sewn mattress made out of straw and covered with a dull-colored cotton fabric. The small hut with its thatched roof had inside walls caked with deep red clay and decorated with interesting patterns in white chalk. The door, standing slightly ajar, and the windows that let in the bright light of late morning, were made out of weathered wood that had lost its shine. The earthen floor of this simple hut was partially covered by a mat woven from tree bark and pieces of fabric. In the small area designated as a kitchen were clay pots, plates, and cups. A large pot of water with a spout crafted in the shape of a fish had a few droplets that drizzled down its sides. Right by it was a small brick furnace, with bright orange embers still burning. The sweet smell of cooked rice and lentils wafted from the steaming pot that sat on top.

Sita felt a wave of relief and gratitude at this sudden and unexpected turn of events. Once again, warm tears laced her beautiful black eyes as her mind shuffled back and forth between relief for what was present and a stabbing pain for all she had lost. She lay still while scenes from her past flitted by in her memory. In her mind's eye she saw the large bedroom with its intricately carved bed made of rosewood, the soft cushions with silk embroideries depicting heroic battles and festivities upon which she and Rama had spent many a carefree night in each other's delightful company. The immaculate garden lined with rose bushes and fruit trees where she lingered every evening, with his strong arms around her, attentively listening to every word she said. The vivid smell of the market streets with their array of vendors calling out for attention and the rush of colorfully dressed citizens who would wave and throw flowers as she rode by in her chariot. The temple by the lake, housing the great bath where women of the royal family gathered to bathe in its cool waters and chat as they laughed about everything that amused them. All seemed to have disappeared, faded like a dream, and she felt transported not to wakefulness but to another dream, the dream of waking up in the hermitage of a renowned sage who endorsed a lifestyle completely different from what she was accustomed to. She felt alone and abandoned, with not one familiar face, and yet safe in the comfort of complete strangers who had opened up their hearts and home for her.

With the vague fatigue of burdensome gratitude that coaxes the unwilling spirit to place one weary footstep before the other, Sita felt something like nausea, a desire to spit out the life within her. Yet even this task demanded a strength she lacked, as she struggled to even stir in her bed. An internal cesspool of endless darkness held her tightly and seemed to prohibit hope of any kind. She was weary of life that flowed along indifferent to the unavoidable longings of those it carried forth with it mercilessly. In brief moments when she allowed herself to feel, it was as if fragments of her were falling apart, not in chunks but like dust being blown away to reveal nothing more than other layers of dust underneath.

"I have been saved! Saved by the great sage Valmiki and forced to make sense of my life all over again!" she whispered. Her voice bore a deep tone of disappointment.

Her memory jogged back to the many brand-new beginnings she had experienced in the duration of her still-young life. At the tender age of sixteen, she had to leave her father's home to be the young wife to the crown prince, Rama, who lived with an enormous family that she barely knew. The difficult task of figuring out alliances and loyalties to survive the intricate politics of royalty demanded that she exercise every bit of wisdom within her command. Just as Sita had settled into the new normal of life as a married woman, Rama's father King Dasharatha exiled him to the forest for a lengthy period of fourteen years. Sita had pleaded with Rama to take her along, fearful of being left behind in a home that would never feel like home without him. Rama had conceded.

With that, Sita had experienced another new beginning, living in the forest with her husband. Though the conditions of her life there had seemed hard, Sita deeply cherished this episode! Left alone without the encumbrances of princely rituals and the craftiness of ambitious family, she and Rama had each discovered love in its truest form. For the first time in their still-new life together, she saw her husband as a vulnerable young man, pretenses peeled away in the expansiveness of the unexplored forest. And he, in turn, had discovered that Sita was more than just a wife; she was a lively, intelligent, passionate woman with a heart filled with innocent longing for love and understanding. This new life in the harsh forest with scanty possessions had enriched their souls as each of them blossomed in the warm sunshine of their mutual love. Sita had everything that she had longed for in a companion and had secretly wished their life in the forest would never end. But wicked destiny had different plans for the young couple. Thirteen years had passed.

Ravana, king of Lanka, filled with pride and envy, had cunningly abducted young Sita and placed her in his palace lawn like a distasteful memento reminding him of his ugly conquest. Disguised as a saint seeking alms, he had come by the hut that beloved Rama had constructed for her in the forest. With Rama gone away, hunting for deer, Sita had felt compelled to provide alms for a begging ascetic.

Just as she had stepped out of the hut, shrewd Ravana had grabbed her and forced her into his chariot. Her pleas fell on deaf ears as, lust-filled and ravenous, he had dragged her into his kingdom. Here too she had endured the new beginning of relentless humiliation and the torment of his advances upon her, which she had thwarted. Everything sacred had been destroyed. The illustrious woman with a beautiful mind and kind heart was reduced to the status of a seductive toy in his cruel hands.

She had given up all hope for happiness, first becoming reserved and then withdrawing from life like someone robbed of a soul. But her beloved Rama had come back for her; he had waged a historic battle, slain the evil Ravana, and taken her back with open arms and fresh vows of love. Her heart had hungered for him with such intense longing that she blossomed once again under his protective care.

Soon fourteen years had passed, and Rama and Sita were thrilled to return to Ayodhya as King and Queen.

So there it was, another new beginning as queen to the great King Rama, who having expanded his empire by slaying Ravana, ruled with impeccable justice and fairness. Here, too, their happiness was short-lived. Rumors abounded as people questioned her chastity – questions that came about because of the time she had spent as captive in Ravana's palace. At first Rama ignored the rumors and tried to mend matters with a greater display of love towards her. But while Sita's heart was ready to grow and move forward, Rama's giving had reached its limit. Their love, needing the wholesomeness of daily bread, grew distasteful in the richness of palace life. Even though Sita was pregnant with their child, their minds were riddled with conflicting loyalties, causing their hearts to grow apart in silence. Rama had finally succumbed to the influence of rumors and dispatched her to the forest, his precious wife, whose innocence he could not prove even though he knew of it.

And now, in a bizarre twist of events, she found herself in the hermitage of the great sage. Sita felt like her faith in humans was completely eroded! There are those who bear their grief by powering through it with a pure strength, like forceful rivers eroding the mountains and plains. There are others who submit to grief as if submitting to an illness that makes its way unheeded and unchallenged, slowly crawling into their innermost being, assimilating with them, and leaving only when it has had its fill. But there are others to whom grief is a violence done to them. Challenging their very faith, it invokes in them the need to depart from every form of life, as they know it, changing them forever.

Sita felt repulsed by her faith. Her faith in Rama, a man she loved, a man who had showered upon her immense joy and happiness, a man who had protected her. This was a man she felt great pride in addressing as husband – and yet he had behaved so very ordinarily!

Deeply exhausted, lost to herself and infinitely saddened, Sita surrendered once again to sleep, which came quickly, kissing her troubled mind and covering her within its blanket of safety.

The woman entrusted with Sita's care had returned. She tucked Sita under a covering and once again took her place right beside her bed. She would see to it that this soon-to-be mother would eat, drink, and rest and be allowed to grieve her losses over the next several days. The woman was sure Sita would come around to their way of life and their way of being at her own pace. Slowly but surely, she would once again cherish life and living. This was, after all just another new beginning

✕

III.

QUEST

Many expressed curiosity about Valmiki's origins. As they spun tales about him, people also pondered the source of his genius. They felt that he was somehow privileged and capable of accessing greater truths. They flocked to his hermitage to learn from him.

To Valmiki their quest for the truth was simply natural. Even the least sensitive of humans questioned the meaning of the world and the reasons behind its functioning – at least in passing – even if they were not driven by vague longings to somehow unearth the truth for themselves. But the presumption that he was closer to such knowledge felt ridiculous.

Valmiki smiled in secret.

For those who wondered about his origins, Valmiki could probably name a few of his ancestors, but nothing beyond that. Besides, how far back did the answer lie? And, even if there was an answer, what was its certainty? Why did it matter? It did not! To him, ancestry remained a matter of no great concern, and therefore he chose neither to add value nor to mitigate in any manner the suspicions of those whose minds were troubled by origins, either of him or of the world. As a matter of fact, he chose to let matters be, without approving or disputing the many rumors. To a few, that was wisdom – and to many more, it was secrecy.

Valmiki wondered. After all, who knew the origins of this world, this universe, and this magnificent creation that we wake up to every morning? Who were they, the pretentious saints who claimed to know the creator as well as they knew a friend or a relative? These Gods who came into existence only after this magnificent creation – how could they know about that which had already existed before them? Who is he, the One who rules from the heavens? Does he know or does he not know these origins that we all clamor to understand?

In keeping with tradition, the discourse had begun in the hermitage. Sages, learned scholars, and students were visiting from all over; and the atmosphere was filled with intense energy. Homes and courtyards were swept and cleaned; mats were spread out below the great banyan. People with diverse goals sat around in a circle, eager to listen and participate. Guests were offered a concoction of curds, butter, honey and milk to consume at the start of each session. Simple food – in line with what was seasonally available – was prepared and served to everyone at the end of the discourse.

This day's topic was related to the origin of the universe, and several participants were eager to learn the mind of the revered sage.

Valmiki began with a Sanskrit verse from the Vedas, in an even yet forceful voice.

नासदासीनोसदासीत्तदानीं नासीद्रजो नो व्योमापरो यत् ।
किमावरीव: कुहकस्यशर्मन्नभ: किमासीद्गहनं गभीरम् ॥
nāsádāsīnno sadāsīttadānīm nāsīdrajo no vyómā paro yat |
kimāvárīvah kuha kasyaśarmannabha kimāsīdgahanam gabhīram ||

In the very beginning, there was neither existence nor was there nothingness! Perhaps, there was no air, nor the heavens beyond it. The cosmic waters in the depths from which we assume the world emerged, under whose power did it exist? What covered it? Where was it?

—

न मृत्युरासीदमृतं न तर्हि न रात्या आन्ह आसीत् प्रकेत: ।
आनीदवातं स्वधया तदेकं तस्माद्धान्यन्नपर: किंचनास ॥
na mrityurāsīdamritam na tarhi na rātryā ahná āasīt praketah |
ānīdavātam svadhayā tadekam tasmāddhānyanna parah kiñcanāsa ||

Then, there was neither immortality nor was there death. Neither was there night nor was there day. There was just that 'One', who was self-sustaining and who perhaps breathed without air.

—

तम आसीत्तमसा गूळ्हमग्रे प्रकेतं सलिलं सर्वमा इदम् ।
तुच्छेनाभ्वपिहितं यदासीत्तपसस्तन्महिना जायतैकम् ॥
tama āasīttamasā gūhamagre praketam salilam sarvamā idam |
tucchyenābhvapíhitam yadāsīttapasastanmáhinā jāyataikam ||

In the beginning there was perhaps just darkness surrounded by darkness. Perhaps the world was filled with invisible waters and the 'One' hidden in nothingness arose as a result of heat!

———

कामस्तदग्रे समवर्तताधिमनसो रेत: प्रथमं यदासीत् ।
सतोबन्धुमसतिनिरविन्दन्हृदिप्रतीष्या कवयो मनीषा ॥
kāmastadagre samavartatādhimanaso retah prathamam yadāsīt |
sato bandhumasatini ravindan hṛdi pratīsyā kavayó manīshā ||

Possibly desire came upon the 'One'! Desire, which I assume was the primal seed born out of the mind. There are sages who have sought such wisdom in their hearts, and they know that which is aligned to the nature of the 'one' and that which is not.

———

तिर्श्चीनो विततो रश्मीरेषामध: स्विदासी ३ दुपरिस्विदासीत् ।
रेतोधा आसन्महिमान् आसन्तृत्स्वधा आवस्तात् प्रयति: परस्तात् ॥
tiraścīno vitato raśmireāmadhah svidāsī 3 duparisvidāsīt |
retodhā āasanmahimāná āasantsvadhā āvastātprayatih parastāt ||

And they have stretched out their minds, to know what was above, know what was below, what were those crucial powers and what were those forces that brought in fertility? These sages assume that perhaps, lying below was strength and lying above was impulse!

———

को आद्धा वेद क इह प्रवोचत् कुत आअजाता कुत इयं विसृष्टि: ।
अवट्द्रिवा आस्य विसर्जनेनाथाको वेद यत आबभूव ॥

ko addhā véda ka iha pravócat kutá āajātā kutá iyam visrishtih |
arvāgdevā asya visárjanenāthāko veda yata āababhūvá ||

Then again, who knows? Who can say with certainty how and when this creation happened? The Gods themselves have arrived after creation, so who can truthfully know when it all began?

———

इयं विसृष्टिर्यत आबभूव यदिवा दधेयदिवा न ।
यो आस्याध्यक्ष: परमे व्योमन्त्सो आंग वेद यदिवा न वेद ॥
iyam visrishtiryatá āabahūva yadivā dadheyadivā na |
yo asyādhyáksah parame vyómantso anga veda yadivā na veda ||

Perhaps even the 'One' who is present in the heavens is unaware of when he designed or if he designed creation. Maybe he knows – or maybe even he does not know all of the answers.

———

The participants were deeply stunned! Valmiki had brilliantly included all theories regarding the origin of the universe, excluding none, yet he had neither confirmed one theory nor disputed the other. As such, each person was free to choose what he wished to believe and everyone remained hesitant.

Valmiki then continued, "Such questioning is suffering in itself! If we were intended to know the truth, then we would have known it by now. Dwelling on these incomprehensible issues and purporting pseudo theories takes us away from our lives. With self-compassion we can soften those hard and unyielding parts of us that encourage us to dwell in the darkness."

Valmiki paused as he gazed into the eyes of his fellow participants. There was silence all around: a few of the sages had tears in their eyes. Valmiki's face was soft as he continued unhurriedly, "We need compassion to deal with the suffering of a mind unable to accept its impotence before the glory of the unknown, we need to practice compassion towards the sufferings of beings whose lives are consumed by their own servitude to their questioning minds. Knowing is like witnessing a beautiful sunset; one can be awed by it or lose out on those precious moments while debating its magnificence."

Brugu, an elderly sage known for his keen scientific reasoning, sat across from Valmiki in the circle. His thin, emaciated body revealed his ribs and spine; his matted hair, tied and twisted, sat like a huge nest on top of his thin frame. He smiled as he spoke in a soft voice that hid his surprise, "You have a way of silencing me, dear Valmiki. I always look forward to your company. Every now and then I forget how small and inconsequential I am, but you put me right back in my place. I thank you for sharing your wisdom with kindness."

A few of the students, eager to display their own thinking, were formulating questions to pose even before they had heard the whole argument. After sage Brugu's confession, everyone fell quiet. It was time to ponder on what they had received. Since no theory had been proposed, there was nothing that would be disintegrated by their questioning.

There remained other topics of discussion. The discourse prolonged into late afternoon. Lemonade and water were served periodically to the participants who sat patiently in the shade of the banyan under the blazing afternoon sun.

Soon it was time to end the discourse. Palms folded at their chests, the participants took turns expressing their regard and gratitude to each other. If differences had emerged and tempers had flared, this was the opportunity to put aside the differences and come together. They all then enjoyed a simple meal that was served with great love. They thanked Valmiki for his hospitality as they left the hermitage feeling grateful!

Afternoon turned to evening, and the birds were flying back home. The reddish orange rays of the sun filtered through branches of trees, powdering the peaceful hermitage with gold-colored dust. Valmiki, tired from the day's activity, sat down upon the landing of a set of stone steps that led to the courtyard. He rested his hand upon his knee, rubbing gently with his body turned to one side. He closed his eyes as he came back to his breath that seemed to be anchored. His chest expanded and contracted slowly as his eyes opened and his gaze turned peacefully to the surrounding garden. The sensation returned! He felt assimilated – to the drooping rose that had fully unfurled and was readying to die; to the tender shoot, green and still-shy, peeking its head out of the red soil; to the leaves that shook with each gentle breeze that drifted among lofty branches; to the echo of the river that flowed unperturbed as he felt his small yet valuable life with gratitude.

Valmiki smiled as he recalled the words of the renowned sage Brugu. There were those he knew, himself among them, whose hearts and minds had been assimilated into the whole like a river embraced by the sea. To them there was no hierarchy to life, no superiority amongst races, no power given to any particular gender, no hesitance to respect all life in every form, no body that was separate from the whole, no sin or virtue that was shameful or great.

Thus, having experienced deep assimilation, Valmiki had gained the ability to feel the pain of all suffering creatures. He felt the pain of the female bird that cried out as her mate was put to death by a heartless hunter, the pain of the leaves that fell off the tree as they died, the pain of animals dragged to their death by predators – feeling each pain as if it were his own, without distinction between himself and the other. And this caused him to embrace and protect all those caught in the seemingly endless river of desperation. He did not question, nor did he judge, the existence and actions of those to whom he provided refuge. More importantly, he did not question or judge his own self harshly either. He had deeply accepted the person he was. He paid attention to his life as it was happening and lived with grace and freedom.

The founding principle of his hermitage had been compassion. Starting out with just a cluster of huts upon the banks of the Tamasa, Valmiki's hermitage had grown slowly over the years. At its founding, he had laid down a code of principles, which guided the affairs of the hermitage. Through the years the hermitage had remained open to all. Those making their way in were provided with a unique opportunity to embrace that, which was sacred. Many had come, and some had left, while those who had no reason to leave chose to stay on forever. Soon this small patch of land was occupied by several huts with walls built of wood caked with mud and roofs of dried leaves. It provided a sanctuary to those who had been outcast, trodden upon, and discarded as useless. This place provided knowledge for all those seeking it, and had become an abode for Godly compassion.

He was not alone! He never could have accomplished this by himself. There were those who understood and followed him in full faith, like his beloved wife and a handful of devoted disciples. There were those who did not have the breadth of understanding that he possessed, yet held to their unshakable faith in his being; they too stayed on and served – to the fullness of their capacity – their master, their teacher and their friend.

The hermitage attracted the attention of those seekers who had been dismayed; it caught the attention of kings and rulers who needed advice; and it enjoyed good repute in the world. And yet this sage, this saint, this human, made it a point to rediscover and re-examine himself over and over again simply to avoid ego-driven stagnation. The universe felt great gratitude in recognizing how Valmiki's earnest reflection was akin to its own!

It had been two whole weeks since Sita had arrived at the hermitage. A majority of her time had been spent within the hut that had become her home. Valmiki had been informed that Sita's morose spirit was slowly recovering, that she had begun to care for herself, bathe, get dressed, clean out her dwelling and partake of her meals on time. But her heart was still aching and she remained incapable of interacting without tear-filled outbursts.

"May she be filled with peace!, May she be reminded of the beauty of her own nature! May she be free from suffering! May she be a source of healing in the world!", Valmiki whispered with closed eyes.

IV.

TARU

S ita felt as if the air was filled with wild and ecstatic joy. The presence of near and dear ones filled the atmosphere with comfort and deep contentment. She heard laughing, endless and infectious. She was a toddler again, running around playing with her cousins and friends in the palace gardens of her father, King Janaka. Into her vision came the lily pond with its exotic blossoms and entrancing mist, offering a path made of soft lily pads she could flit across to reach the other side. Sita felt her tender, soft feet running confidently towards the very first lily pad. Her hair was tied in a neat braid, and her outfit of bright red complemented her dark skin. Laughing loudly, she was filled with a sense of safety as she jumped on the lily pad, not noticing in the least that it still stayed afloat even after she leapt ahead to the next. Her steps were confident and her feet grew in size as she felt herself as she had been – as a young girl, a teenager, and a newly married bride.

Then suddenly she froze. The laughter stopped, the companions disappeared, the mist around the pond grew thick, and the darkness of the surrounding woods grew even deeper. At first she felt nothing, and then a muddy fear grabbed her, as an endless pit seemed to open inside her, heightening her sense of being alone. Fear stirred rapid circles. She felt nauseous and light-headed.

Looking at the lily pad ahead, she now felt deeply uncertain about placing her feet upon it, certain that she would drown in the pond and die. She turned back, and all the previous lily pads that she had darted upon had disappeared. The eerie silence of her surroundings heightened the intensity of her angst, and her insignificance in the context of the world felt imposing and painful. It all began to close in;

the deep dark woods, lifeless and without a sound, grew denser and crawled into the pond.

Sita had to rush forward, but she had no faith! Though she hurriedly decided to move ahead, with her next step she slipped into an abyss, an endless pit, crying out in a voice that felt as vacant as her sinking body.

With that, Sita woke from her nightmare!

Her breathing was rapid; sweat streamed down her face and neck. The wooden door of her hut, though standing ajar, acted as a flimsy barrier between her and the voices that she heard in the distance. Three weeks had passed since her arrival at the hermitage of the great sage. She was safe, and yet grief about her abandonment continued to flood her from nowhere. Instantaneously, her mind had travelled to the unpleasant events of her past, and the story that she had woven around those events were replayed in her mind, just as she had rehearsed them several times. The narrative triggered all-too-familiar feelings of being unlovable and unworthy of kindness.

An excruciating pain gripped her as she cried bitterly. Little did she realize that she was harming her own self by repeating, over and over, the very same tale, memorizing self-woven details that only pushed her further down into the pit of sorrow. She had trusted and expected those around her to care for her wellbeing without ever being told that she had the primary responsibility of care towards the self. However, like every story that has run its course and turns impotent, the plot was losing her interest as her spirit clamored for new reasons to thrive and exist. And all the while, the fresh life within her belly was creating an anticipation of comfort, even though she remained too scared to acknowledge it at times!

Answering a knock, Sita opened the door to find a group of women from the hermitage standing by with smiles that were warm and welcoming. Their colorful saris spoke of simplicity and calm elegance. Their hair was tied in thick braids or pulled back into buns. They smelt of flowers and herbs, and their gazes were filled with kindness. They inquired if she was comfortable and wished her well! This simple act cleared her skies of darkness, and the dense clouds magically disappeared.

Without knowing these generous women, without being known to them, she had somehow established camaraderie – as millions of people do – finding strength in the simple comforts of co-existence. Her heart felt lighter, and she had a lingering sense of being cared for long after they were gone! Perhaps the universe had softly ushered her into a brand-new beginning, despite the fears that lingered in her mind!

Pretty soon, Sita's grief settled down into a steady yet dull presence. Gone, now, was the hope she had once entertained that Rama would come back for her. She felt as if the door of destiny had slammed shut in her face and some raptor, with its ugly talons, had extracted the bits of confidence that lingered. Her eyes were dry; all tears had been shed. A knot of anger entwined itself tightly around her gentle heart, and she refused to smile at memories of the past that had once brought her happiness. Internal rage, powered by self-pity, stayed within her like a pit of fire lit in honor of brutal suffering, warning those who might come too close that she was capable of burning them. Indifference formed a scab over her gravely injured heart, and she went about her day as mechanically as the sun rises and sets unseen, when eyes are blind to its beauty.

Yet even in times of intense grief, life produces moments of unnoticed joy, and her life was sprinkled with these too. The young children of the hermitage visited her often, curious about this gorgeous woman who was amongst them. Somehow the word had gotten out that she was a brilliant storyteller with several interesting tales to narrate. Sita received a steady flow of young visitors who came by everyday, longing to be entertained. She allowed them both within her home and her heart, cherishing their visits as a welcome distraction from the tedium of her routine. But her heart was still a bit heavy. She failed to realize that all had not been lost, and therefore she placed no value on the laughter that came her way as she tended to these young ones.

Taru, a wide-eyed, bright-faced little girl of six years had taken a strong liking to Sita; she did so in the manner of a child, for reasons unknown and without any hesitation in her heart. She came running to the mud hut where Sita sat in silence, bursting in with overflowing excitement, impossible to contain. Hesitating only a minute to catch her breath, she took Sita's hand and spoke quickly and rapidly about something that had to be witnessed that very instant. Sita had no choice other than to accompany Taru.

The little girl dragged Sita along – her tiny body showing surprising strength – into the thickness of the woods. They stopped just a few feet away from a huge anthill. Taru put her index finger on her lips and bid Sita to be quiet as she pointed out a team of angry red ants working hard to carry a ripe plum, half-eaten by the birds, into their anthill. Slowly but surely, the ants were taking turns pushing away at this fruit that would feed them all, until at last they dropped it into the largest opening of their reddish-brown hill.

Sita and Taru stood in silence and observed. The rest of the world around and within them had fallen silent. There was an army of ants surrounding the fruit, each doing their part to make sure they remained safe. Their collective objective was accomplished with commendable precision. A long trail of assistants followed the fast-working army to provide backup in case the need should arise. Another trail of ants preceded the army as if clearing the path for their heroes. A few others scurried around announcing the excitement and cheering their comrades. An enormous smile came upon the child's face as she looked into Sita's eyes. Sita was smiling brightly, too!

For a moment her mind was freed from its incessant recitation of her suffering, and that moment brought great relief within her. The cool woods, the array of life within it, the laughter of the brooks that flowed carelessly, the chirping of birds and the scent of fire that wafted from the hermitage refreshed her senses, making her body feel light, even with the life within it. She forgot about herself and was soon enticed into a long conversation about all the wonderful things that could be discovered around the hermitage.

With Taru leading the way, Sita took her first walk around this new land that had become her home. She noted with deep respect that the residents of the hermitage showed great discipline, were austere, hardworking, and extremely simple. The huts, surrounded by small gardens and courtyards, were all swept clean and kept immaculate. There were shelters constructed for domesticated animals that were protected and cared for. Without social status or ranking amongst the inhabitants, they lived with the preceptor as equals.

Taru pointed out the big banyan; in its shade, every day lessons were conducted in an open classroom. She mentioned enthusiastically that she was a good student and that all her teachers loved her deeply. Sita was delighted to note how girls and women were equals with boys and men in the learning process. An erudite scholar herself, she began to think of ways in which she could be useful to the citizens of this hermitage.

A group of women sat in the distance, separating grains of rice from their husks. They chatted casually and hummed tunes as they worked. Their labor was interspersed with laughter and kind greetings from the men who passed by them. Guru-Ma, the wife of sage Valmiki, looking radiant with her shining grey hair and soft brown skin, sat in their midst. Her face was wrinkled appealingly in places where her skin had been creased by her enchanting smile. Not only was she Valmiki's mentor and guide, she also served as a confidant and friend to all the women of the hermitage. They respected her tremendously, and she treated them with utmost kindness.

A woman sitting by Guru-Ma nudged her arm and pointed in the direction where Taru and Sita could be seen walking together. Guru-Ma exchanged silent glances with others in the group, and they smiled softly. Each bore a history that was part painful and part filled with joy, but what held them together was their understanding of each other's suffering and their suspension of judgment of each other. They smiled, knowing that they would welcome yet another member into their tribe soon enough, though not just yet. Seeing young Sita's beautiful smile brought tears into the eyes of Guru-Ma, who served as mother to all other women in the hermitage and took delight in this small transformation she was witnessing in Sita.

It was time for the Sun to set. The sky, dressed in glorious reds with tinges of purple, served as a perfect backdrop to this eventful day; it had brought subtle shades of warm delight into Sita's life. The people of the hermitage moved around bidding each other goodbye and concluding yet another day in their peaceful lives. Sita was mesmerized by the sound of voices chanting Sanskrit verses in rhythmic tones that seemed to fill the entire universe with much- needed peace. The hermitage echoed with Om Shanthi, Om Shanthi, Om Shanthi! (May there be peace, may there be peace, may there be peace!).

V.

CONQUEST OR LOVE

Kings made alliances and produced heirs. If love was destined to happen, it strode in and made pleasant that which was already ordained. But what was love? Was it for poets and writers alone? Were princes and kings entitled to a share of this unspoken sentiment? Was it the love for accomplishment that caused them to collect brides like trophies, or was it the soft love of a gentle heart filled with care and desire for another?

King Janaka, the father of Sita, had bedecked his palace in the city of Mithila with flags and flower banners. The hand of his one and only child, princess Sita, was to be given in marriage to the prince who could string the bow presented to him by Shiva, the God of Destruction.

The test for this feat was to be held in the central courtyard of his beautiful palace. Gardens with fountains lined the outer edges of this courtyard. Flower garlands adorned the many columns that surrounded it. Colorful patterns made out of chalk decorated the paths leading to the arena at the center that was lined with seats for the participants. Lamps were lit, and musicians entertained guests who came from all over the world. Princes from various kingdoms gathered in the hope of winning the hand of Sita.

Trumpets were sounded, perfumed waters sprinkled and flowers were thrown as Sita entered the assembly. Rama, the crown prince of Ayodhya, desirous of winning the princess's hand, sat amongst the contestants, confident of his victory. He outshone the others in his youth and remarkably handsome features. Attracted by Rama's sculpted forehead, large brown eyes, distinctive nose, and shoulder-length hair that curled at the edges, Sita cast him a quick glance accompanied by a shy smile as she entered.

That was the first moment Rama had set his eyes upon Sita, who was only sixteen at the time. Her deep black eyes shone from her beautifully carved face, framed with a crown of scented auburn hair decorated with jasmine. She was adorned with bangles upon her wrist, gold necklaces made of precious stones and pearls, and with anklets made out of silver with tiny bells that jingled as she walked slowly into the courtyard. Her golden yellow sari hugged her slender frame and heightened the shine in her dark complexion as her lotus-like lips smiled a tentative smile.

Silence fell among guests and contestants as they watched this young, elegant, and attractive maiden walk amidst them to take her seat beside her father. Rama was mesmerized for a few moments, but quickly regained himself.

Rama dismissed the murmurings of his heart and reminded himself of his objective. He was there to win her hand, of course, but he preferred to think of her as a conquest. After all, as the crown prince of Ayodhya, he was duty bound to bring honor to his land and people. He had been taught well, and had mastered the practice of self-restraint that a prince should exercise. Bred for warfare his mind was trained to rule with fairness and justice, but his heart was ignored. The tender feelings that flowed out of him were dismissed, as they had always been ever since he was a child. Labeled with the tainted star of weakness that would affect his judgment, his feelings were kept in check, governed with pride, and assigned to corners where they were to remain hidden.

But nothing in human nature is redundant, and that which is denied its rightful place can remain buried-alive only so long. It will, at the most inconvenient hour, rear its overbearing and unbridled head with a force unimaginable!

As the assembly settled, King Janaka ordered the bow of Shiva to be brought into the courtyard. The heavy wooden bow carved intricately, was borne upon a carriage pulled along by ten men whose backs were bent in concentrated effort. King Janaka announced that the prince who could string this mighty bow single-handed would be given the hand of Princess Sita.

Many eager princes clamored and rushed to meet the challenge, but were simply crushed. Most could not even pick up the heavy instrument and were mocked by the others in the gathering.

Ravana, the King of Lanka, well known for his pride-filled ego, came forward to string the bow. He was a large-framed man whose face was distinguished by a thick moustache twisted at the ends, and long side burns. He had a huge belly that pressed against the tightly fastened garment covering his lower body, and his garish jewelry made him all the more conspicuous. As he twirled the edges of his moustache and attempted to lift the bow, he had to stop midway, incapable of hoisting the heavy instrument any further. He gritted his teeth and stiffened his jaw as he strained to pick up the bow, and then let out a shout as it slipped and fell back into the carriage. A few chuckles were heard as he stormed out of the courtyard, angered at such humiliation. Quickly glancing at Sita as he hastened past, he was annoyed to see the princess giggling at his failure. He lips curled as he swore he would have his revenge, one way or the other!

Rama, who had waited his turn patiently, stepped forward. The young maidens seated by Sita who served as companions to the princess, whispered his name in her ear as they held their breath and clutched their hands, hoping for his victory. Sita's heart beat wildly and pearls of sweat formed upon her forehead.

Without a second thought, Rama casually lifted the heavy bow and strung it with ease. The bewildered assembly was stunned for a moment before King Janaka proudly announced the victory of the young prince.

The citizens of Mithila, who were delighted at the mastery of Rama, expressed great pride as they declared him their prince and heir. Quickly, the festivities turned into a celebration such as never had been seen before. King Janaka, Sita's father, stepped down from his throne and washed the feet of the young prince with perfumed water. Prince Rama was to wed his precious child and relieve him of his duties towards her as a father. Trumpets blasted, and the drums beat loudly as flowers were showered upon the prince of Mithila and Ayodhya. By simply stringing a bow, Rama had enlarged his kingdom and picked up his bride.

Sita strained her neck to get a good look at her soon-to-be husband, but all she could see was the swarming crowd of kings, ministers, sages, and priests all congratulating the prince who stood with his back to her. A sudden look of sadness crossed her innocent face as she was rushed back to her quarters to prepare for the wedding. Her heart beat loudly in anxious anticipation, and a huge tear formed in her eye; within the next few hours she was to leave her family, home, country, and people.

The young couple held their hands for the first time as they circled the sacred fire acknowledging their duties and responsibilities towards each other. As they went around seven times, they swore to treat each other with respect, to remain a source of strength and courage, to love each other always, to sustain joy and happiness within their lives, to remain truthful, and to always stay by each other's side. They appealed to the almighty God for his blessings for this union. They exchanged garlands made of flowers and were pronounced man and wife.

After the gallant feast and festivities amid tears, hugs, and farewells, Sita followed Rama into his chariot. He wasted no time and thrashed at the horses, eager to show off his new acquisition to his father the King. After all, he, Prince Rama, had successfully accomplished his mission.

Needless to say, his love for her was yet to unfold. Soon his life would change entirely, but he had no idea of the riches of her spirit or of its power to transform him into a man. After all, kings made alliances and produced heirs, but women married for love and made the laughter of children. Sita was young, caring, and open to her new life. Together they strode into Ayodhya, Sita's new home.

And now, some fourteen years later, the promises they had made to each other were conveniently forgotten. Rama had discarded her and his unborn child from his life and empire. Sitting morosely by the window of her hut in the hermitage, Sita gently stroked her swollen belly. She wondered where her true home was. Raised by a strict father who willingly gave her away to a stranger, she was used to being told that, as a woman, she could only be a guest in the home of her father.

Her only home, it was repeated often, would be the one that her husband would provide her. Now ousted by Rama, she felt she had nowhere else to go.

Even as her eyes moistened, her mind recalled the words of kind sage Valmiki when he had first seen her abandoned in the forest. "Cry," he had said, "until you realize that I have been here and never left you!" Sita smiled, as she understood the subtle meaning hidden in his words. "Home is within or not at all!" she whispered softly to herself.

✕

VI.

GURU-MA

The front porch of the humble home of Valmiki and Guru-Ma was open to the star-lit skies. Burning fires at the fire-pit, situated at one end of the rectangular porch, exuded warmth and extended comfort to the old couple.

Gazing at the night sky with its brilliantly lit stars had been a lifelong refuge for Guru-Ma. Draped in an off-white sari tie-dyed in earth red and pale green, she looked graceful and radiant. Her silver grey, long, and voluminous hair had been woven into a bun that was decked with sweet-smelling champak flowers. Though her face was wrinkled, she still had rounded cheeks, a long, graceful neck, and a beautiful jawline. Her pale brown skin reflected the bluish-orange hues of the burning fire, and her slanted eyes shone as she sat upon a mat with her head resting against a pole. Valmiki embraced her warmly as he sat down beside, her and the stillness between them continued, uninterrupted by conversation.

To the world it seemed a rare fortune to live and participate in this seemingly unique partnership. Their mutual love was much envied and the cause of wonder amongst many. What was it really like to live in such a harmonious union? Was is simply luck or was it the result of years of hard work? They had each suffered as individuals, as a couple, as parents, and as folks within a community. This much-envied transition was the result of deep acceptance and surrender.

Neither of them was born to privilege, nor did they have the necessary guidance to know their unique sense of self. Their life together had begun in the community of hunters whose villages and tribes were located in the hilltops farther east from the river Ganges. Married at a young age, they simply followed in the footsteps of their ancestors who had lived their lives, worked their work, and slept their sleep, never asking more from life than what it had to offer.

As a young couple, Guru-Ma and Valmiki had assumed their responsibilities wholly, giving to the Gods what belonged to the Gods and partaking in all the religious and social aspects of their community. They had simply expected that their lives would follow the path laid out by their forefathers. If, deep down in the hidden trenches of their hearts, they did possess morbid feelings to discover their own self, they were simply not aware of them. Neither were they blind to the beauty of life around, nor did they feel any deep-seated need to figure out life and its workings.

Married at the age of eighteen, they had started off as newlyweds in a home that was one amongst a cluster situated in the outer periphery of the village inhabited by their tribe. Like all other homes in this community, theirs was constructed with carved wood and hay. The entrance was decorated with the head of a tiger that had been hunted and killed by Valmiki, one of the best hunters in the community. Their possessions were meager, restricted to the essentials. Other than a few sets of clothing, housewares, and bedding, their home was barren of material comforts. Living in complete conformity with the practices of their tribe, they soon produced two boys and a baby girl.

Dressed in a head gear made out of canine teeth and clothing made of animal skin, Valmiki left each morning with his spear, blade, and bow and arrow to hunt for animals in the forest. Guru-Ma promptly observed her role as wife, mother, and breadwinner to the family of five. She tended to their three children – two boys aged three and two and a newborn baby girl – even as she completed her household chores and wove cloth that was sold in the villages in exchange for food and household articles. Surrounded by family and community, they lived a life of relative ease.

On one fateful day, young Valmiki was returning home carrying a fine stag that he had killed in the forest when he ran into the Seven Sages meditating peacefully. Adorned in white robes, their matted hair tied firmly behind their heads, they sat with their eyes closed in deep contemplation. Part innocently and part arrogantly, Valmiki called out after them loudly, offering a portion of his kill to the emaciated sages. He warned them of the dangers present in the forest and offered to protect them while they remained in the dreaded jungle.

The compassionate sages gently refused his offer of meat and, though unarmed, seemed indifferent to the perils that they were warned about. Surprised by the strangeness of their demeanor, Valmiki stayed on, observing their habits and questioning them inquisitively! He was taken aback by the calmness of their disposition, their lack of clamoring, their capacity to sit quietly in meditation, the scanty food that they ate contentedly, their need to do good unto others, their indifference regarding death, and the faith that caused them to pursue an existence that was not governed by fear. In an instant, an obscure, long-forgotten need that had been buried deep within the innumerable folds of his existence came alive! Suddenly he desired to know the truth regarding the meaning of life, the purpose of existence, and the way to lasting happiness. Just as soon as this seemingly harmless desire launched itself into his heart, he squashed it out of deep fear – the fear that such thinking was sure to destroy his precious family that depended on him.

But it was an idea preordained by destiny, and even he could not possibly prevent it. He suddenly realized that he had lived his entire youth like a frog in a well, assuming the well to be the whole world. He realized how little he knew and how much more there was for him to learn.

Valmiki had assumed incorrectly that he had it all. He was, after all, the best hunter in his community, his life was comfortable, there was an abundance of wild life to hunt in the forest, and he had a family that loved him deeply. And yet he lacked faith. He lacked the ability to feel safe when posed with the uncertainties of life, he did not possess the knowing that enabled these sages to lean into the unknown with complete faith that they would be cared for. He was ignorant of the ways in which he could instill steadiness in his consciousness, and he could not fully comprehend the ability of these sages to care for others in the same manner as they cared for their own selves. He wondered what it was like to feel sufficient in one's own self, to not fear death, and to trust that life will surely bring with it the strength needed to deal with the ambiguities it offers.

Valmiki had gone back home and narrated his experience with the Seven Sages to Guru-Ma. He had hoped secretly that she would somehow sense his urgency to realize the truth and would dissuade him from pursuing it. He hoped that being around his family would crush this overwhelming desire that had come to life in him. But going back home had only strengthened his craving that could not be overcome.

Guru-Ma had listened to him inattentively, as she was consumed in the act of providing care for the young ones and preparing meals for the family. It did not occur to her, even in passing, that he was desperately trying to stop himself from leaving them to find his true self and the truth of life. When their young sons argued and bickered about the rightful owner of a shining rock, Guru-Ma hoped that Valmiki would intervene and put an end to their screaming and shouting. But Valmiki had continued on with his story about the Seven Sages. Tired and irritated, Guru-Ma had snapped at the boys and chased them out. She absent-mindedly served Valmiki his evening meal, not imagining even for a moment that it would be the last meal they would share together for a long time to come.

Rushing to feed the newborn baby girl, she left Valmiki by the corner of their kitchen floor, deep in thought and indifferent to his surroundings. Even after she safely tucked in the young one, she turned around to find Valmiki frozen to his spot, his plate of food untouched.

A sudden surge of anger overtook her. "Do you think the seven sages will feed and care for your family, you fool?" she had asked in fury. Having managed to capture his attention, she continued, "Will the truth put clothes on our backs? Will it weave cloth and take it to the market? Will this truth draw water from the well and skin the animals? Will it at-least keep your sons from squabbling incessantly or our newborn from crying? Of what use is it – this truth – that you ignore the food before you and sit there staring at nothing, while there is so much work to be done!"

Guru-Ma knew she had gone a bit too far in her reproach, but the damage was already done!

"I kill animals, innocent animals, every day to provide for this family! The sages tell me that killing is sinful! Will you and the kids share in my sins just as I share the meat with you?" Valmiki had asked in a trembling voice.

Still furious, frustrated at his relentless introspection, Guru-Ma responded even more harshly in a voice that seethed with anger, "No, your sins are yours alone! Why would we partake in your sinning?"

He had stared at her like a waylaid man looking for a path out of the deep woods. She had walked away, looking for the boys who seemed to have disappeared. She noted as she walked that she would have to talk to him about these Seven Sages sometime later, at a more peaceful moment!

It was not as if their love had gone sour! It was not even that he was uncaring! But somehow the bliss of wedded life had altogether disappeared, and each of them felt like they had stumbled into a world of endless caring, providing, nurturing, and being available constantly! This life they had together felt like a sudden expansion, the kind that did not allow for their nest to grow slowly in anticipation of the change that was yet to come. Instead, it felt as if life had pulled out their nest holding it carelessly at the edges in an effort to make it supple and ready for the young ones to bounce in. But in the process it had torn out holes that rudely allowed the elements to come inside.

Suddenly the newlyweds who had shared every detail of every day could barely find time to acknowledge each other as they fell asleep exhausted. The thick tedium of life seemed to close in around them, drawing them deeper and deeper into an endless hole. Even if they were sure that they would emerge from it, years would be clipped from their lives and feathers would be clipped off their wings. Under the heavy weight of this surmounting burden, Valmiki felt sure he would be crushed, unfulfilled, unrealized, and lost forever.

Valmiki was gone before daybreak. He had left Guru-Ma and the children to go in search of the truth. Guru-Ma's heart was heart no longer. Her grief, it seemed, had invited clusters of wild ravens, as black and forbidding as a cloudy sky, to descend upon her forever. Her heart felt ravaged as if the ravens were picking at her, nibbling the flesh, puncturing holes, and gnawing at the tatters left behind. She wore her sorrow mercilessly. She fought to hide away, avoiding unwanted attention from neighbors and strange men. She fought to keep her children within her sight and struggled to raise them in the light of their own internal marking. She fought with her own self about what she could and could not be for her needy family.

Feeling lonely and isolated in Valmiki's absence, Guru-Ma had attempted to kill herself and had failed. When nothing changed and life continued stubbornly, refusing to yield, compelled by her need to provide and nurture, she had found the strength to survive. Suffering, even unimaginable suffering, becomes tolerable when there is meaning – and what greater meaning did she need for her own suffering than her desire to simply be present for her children?

Soon a whole year had passed since Valmiki had left, and Guru-Ma suspended whatever hope she had harbored for his return.

The youngest of their three beautiful children, Manu the baby girl – doted upon by her older brothers – was ready to take her first steps. Holding onto the legs of a brother, she got to her feet, curiously aware of her new undertaking. The little one looked up at her brother's face with its bright smile then looked over at her mother who was surprisingly attentive and not preoccupied. Then, making a leap of faith, she took her first steps towards Guru-Ma. She cried as she stumbled to the ground, a cry that was a mixture of fear and the thrill of accomplishment. Guru-Ma found herself smiling with pride, her first smile in a very long time. A silent resolve to protect her children crept into her body, bringing with it a steely strength that combined fearlessness and a sense of freedom.

She decided to build a world of her own, one step at a time, led by an internal compass that she had forgotten she possessed. No longer belonging to a man she could rely on, she learned to belong to her own self. Even in the trenches of gravest despair, she had discovered the unique strength of the newly liberated; to whom the world is but a treasure trove – a place where each person does what is necessary to find a way to live. All that which was crucial to the preservation of life had assumed priority.

At the end of a hard day, as her children slept in the hut they called home, she watched them with wonder – wonder at their resilience, wonder at their tenacity, wonder at their kindness, and wonder at the strong bonds of family she had created. Her love for them would help tide her over these seemingly unconquerable hardships. Was it fair that she had to raise them single handedly? Perhaps not! Was it fair that Valmiki had left her at this inconvenient hour to find himself? Perhaps not! But like a creature in nature that lives its life fully, never regretting, never filled with self-pity, never brooding over its plight, never drawing comparisons, simply existing as magnificently as it can and striving for the best life it can make for itself, Guru-Ma, too, somewhere plowing along the tenacious path of her life, had slowly accepted it fully.

As she gained strength, her anger faded, the rage melted away, and what was left behind was not a heart-hardened woman shunned and aggrieved, but a compassionate one who was kind and sufficient. What her husband had gone away to seek, she had had to find within herself right there, in the thick bustle of her life and amidst her needy children, and she had succeeded.

Two whole years after Valmiki left, there came a fortunate day – a day when Guru-Ma was gathering firewood for her family – when she saw him once again. He was standing with his arms raised and palms folded under the wild spread of an ambitious banyan tree. His eyes were closed in deep meditation, his hair matted and dirty, his body depleted, and the bones protruded dangerously on his emaciated frame. His face was still haunted with signs of restlessness. So lost was he in his single-minded dedication that he remained in deep meditation, unmindful of the anthill surrounding his feet and legs. The people in the villages nearby considered him a great saint and treated him with utmost reverence.

Guru-Ma had slowly walked up to him and stood before him in silence. For the first time, she saw him for what he was – another human struggling to make sense of his world, unable to live peacefully within its four walls, and also unable to give it all up and die. Her anger no longer flared at the sight of him. He had lost his power over her and she had become sufficient in herself. She half-smiled at the path her own life had assumed; it had caused her so much grief and had brought to her so much joy. Somehow it made sense! It made sense that her soul seemed to flow along a pre-destined path, gathering and attracting experiences that it needed to surrender, so she held absolute faith in the life she had been given. It made sense that life flowed along an unrecognizable course, indifferent to the desires and expectations of those that it carried along. It made sense that a heart open to love and kindness had greater riches to harvest from life than one that was closed with anger. It made sense that when affectionate care was extended towards all creatures crossing your path you were somehow in alliance with the universe and its singular purpose. It made sense that all this clamoring was unnecessary, the pain inflicted upon another was pain inflicted upon the self, and the love extended to another was love towards one's self.

She closed her eyes and looked within. Guru-Ma was at peace, no longer defined by Valmiki. Her sense of self was not defined by his desire for her, she was no longer the woman that he had married; she had grown to gracefully embrace her life fully. She wondered at the million things that seemed to have fallen in place just to bring the two of them together; she realized how everything that she was doing was in fact affecting the lives of so many more people and creatures she would perhaps never meet in her lifetime. She felt assimilated with a purpose much larger and more infinite than her small and seemingly inconsequential life.

She had silently placed a sparse meal of bread, wild berries and a drink of water in front of Valmiki and left. Her footsteps had felt light, and her body had felt airy. There was a radiant smile upon her face, and she had felt the presence of peace within her heart. She had resolved to love her children, not fearing the pain that her attachments would cause nor wanting to run from life in order to make peace with it. Before she had disappeared, she had turned around and wished Valmiki well. She did not hope to see him ever again. But as fate determined, they were to meet again a whole decade later when he returned to her.

Guru-Ma, gazing up at the stars, nestled safely in Valmiki's loving arms in the quiet of the night. The soothing song of a lullaby drifted to her ears, along with the whimpering of an infant from a neighboring home. Soon, quiet fell upon the hermitage once more as the couple shifted gently, relaxing further into each other's embrace. The warm fire crackled and burnt with a familiar hum. The penetrating silence of the night was only broken by the distant moo of a cow.

Guru-Ma's mind instantly travelled back twenty years to that fateful orange-lit morning when Valmiki had come back to her and their children. Busy tending to a newborn calf and her mother, Guru-Ma had not noticed Valmiki watching her attentively from a distance. She was taken by surprise to find his thin, emaciated body standing before her, shuddering violently in the crisp, cold morning air. He had come back! She had fancied this very scene several years before when he had left her alone with their young children. She had rehearsed how she expected to rant and curse him if he were ever to return.

But times had changed! All of her imagined anger had been washed away into some eternal sinkhole of meaninglessness. No longer needy for his love, she was curious about his need to return. But her curiosity had to wait. She had generously offered care as she draped him in her blanket and welcomed him inside to partake of the family's morning meal.

Valmiki had stared at each of his children with surprise and sadness; he had missed watching them grow. The eldest of his three children, Chiru, practically a young man, was a handsome seventeen-year-old. Valmiki recalled how he had been close to that age when he married Guru-Ma. Sumi, his second son, sixteen, was equally handsome and well built. Manu the youngest, a beautiful twelve-year-old girl, smiled shyly at Valmiki as she fidgeted nervously. Valmiki stared with a quiet pride at the broad noses of his children – the hallmark of his own facial feature which each had inherited. On them, this feature seemed more beautiful than it was on him.

Standing in their midst, feeling the awkwardness of a stranger and the brimming love of a parent, he hesitated as he smiled. Without anxiety, Guru-Ma had introduced him and directed her children to welcome him; they had obeyed. Once again she had aided Valmiki by breaking down the barrier between him and their children. But his work was far from done. It would take time and consistent effort to earn back the love that he had simply taken for granted a long time ago.

Valmiki had wondered whether his findings were worth the years he had missed out as a father. He had found what he had left to seek.

He had found enlightenment! He, too, in his long-drawn, elaborate penance and practice of meditation had come to visit the very same place that Guru-Ma now stood, years ahead of him. Except that she had excelled!

She had excelled not in time or in the quality of the experience but in translating her learning into the informality of everyday existence. She had incorporated this unique knowledge into the making of home and hearth, into tending cattle and growing crops, into kindness for strangers and care for her neighbors, into patience in raising her children and savoring her sense of self. She was well versed in living the life that Valmiki could only preach about, and he had come to realize that there was more growth for him in her way, because her way embraced life in its wholesome sense.

A wave of shame flooded him as he had asked her, in a heavy voice punctuated with wild tears and gasps, for forgiveness – forgiveness for his abandonment of her and their young children. She had taken a whole moment before speaking in a soft voice, with the casualness of the kind-hearted, "Only you can forgive yourself! We all suffer and we are all the cause of suffering to others! Be kind to yourself Valmiki!"

On hearing these words, his heart felt filled with gratitude and tears had formed in his eyes! He had laughed aloud at the thought of those many years spent searching all over the world for that which was holed up within his own home. And yet this experience of separation felt somehow essential; it had enabled Valmiki and Guru-Ma to step outside of their assigned roles and find that unique sense of self that had been buried under layers of expectations. Where love can sink, love can rise as well, and Valmiki was determined to find a way into Guru-Ma's heart once more and regain his place as her companion.

With this, a new kind of courtship had begun, one that was more giving and less needy, one that was both fulfilling and safe, one that would forge a partnership based on mutual trust and respect.

After years of struggle and strife that had pulled them apart from each other, somewhere, somehow, and unknowingly they had simply surrendered to life and were surprised to rediscover their love for each other. However, they experienced their relationship quiet differently after this re-union. This time around, the need to be more than what they could possibly be to the other had disappeared altogether. Time apart had enabled the understanding that they each were enough within their own selves, enough for each other, enough for their children and their grandchildren and enough in the context of the larger world. So now they could sit by each other like two completed universes, not wanting, not grasping, not belonging, not possessing, but as the quiet complement of man and woman.

With this, their new life had begun. His vision created the hermitage, while she remained his spiritual guide. Valmiki felt it was imperative to share with the outside world their wisdom while Guru-Ma had continued on her path of self-discovery and inner freedom. He wrote their findings, and she narrated them to him; he gained fame while she gained family. And yet, neither would let themselves be fooled by that which was transient. Here they were, years later, bound in each other's arms, filled with a soothing tranquility while gazing at the night sky.

Valmiki yawned wearily. The fire they had both enjoyed was dying out and it was time to get to bed. "I saw Sita walking with Taru this evening." whispered Guru-Ma. "We should pay her a visit sometime. I remember the hardships that I faced when you left us. She could use a word of encouragement right now." She stood up to enter their home.

"Sure, my dear, you know best and I trust your opinion." spoke Valmiki as he followed his wife inside.

VII

SHELTER

The rain had set in steadily and unrelentingly, bringing great joy to the farmers nearby. Drums were beaten, and people danced upon the wet earth. Loud screams of joy and singing could be heard all day long. Because of the rain, however, the busy pathways of the hermitage were vacant. Even the birds had disappeared behind black clouds that delivered endless sheets of rain.

Sita, now in her last trimester, sat beside the warm furnace in the small mud hut, stringing flowers into garlands. She picked two flowers at a time, set their stems beside each other with the petals facing outward, and knotted the stems together with a piece of string.

She stopped and sighed! It felt ironic that these flowers whose destiny was tied together were facing outward, looking away from each other. A sadness came over her at the thought of her own marriage, which seemed to have taken the path of appeasing those on the outside while Rama and she remained unfulfilled. Her heart ached at the thought of raising Rama's unborn child all by herself.

What if she died giving birth – what then, she wondered? A chill passed down her spine as her hands fell upon her swollen belly in utter helplessness.

Hearing a soft knock at the door of her hut, Sita straightened herself and got to her feet. For a moment she stared at the wooden door, noting how uninterested she was in company or conversation. But it was raining! What if there was someone out there who needed help? She hurried to open the door. Instantly, a bright smile lit up her face. It was Guru-Ma.

"It started to pour heavily all of a sudden Sita! Is it all right for Valmiki and me to take shelter in here for a while? We were just returning from the festivities at the villages nearby. It seems the crowds there have gone wild with joy. The rains have come down at last! Anyhow, we have no desire to be drenched, so is it okay by you if we take shelter in here for a bit? "

"Please do come in! This is your home and the shelter that you have provided me with!" Sita's soft voice was filled with kindness.

Their presence lifted the heaviness of her mood, and a warm energy flowed into the little hut. Sita quickly handed out dry pieces of cloth and blankets to her drenched visitors. While Valmiki settled down by the furnace, warming his feet and rubbing his hands, Guru-Ma seated herself on the mat that was spread out on the floor and pulled a warm blanket tightly around her shoulders.

It had been a little over a month since Sita had moved into this hermitage. Even though Sita had exchanged greetings and good wishes with Valmiki and his wife Guru-Ma on several occasions, this was her first opportunity to spend time alone with the couple. Sita's heart swelled with gratitude for their kindness. With the eagerness of a loving child, she prepared warm milk with cardamom and honey, which she offered to her guests and benefactors.

As the three of them sat silently facing each other, Sita searched for words to break the silence that seemed to prevail. Valmiki was absorbed in studying the flames of the small fire while Guru-Ma sat listening to the downpour beat against the wooden door and window of the small hut. It appeared the two of them were unperturbed by the feeling of awkwardness that now troubled their host.

"For how long do you think it will rain?" Sita asked, relieved that she had found a way to break the silence.

"For as long as it wishes!" Guru-Ma replied unassumingly. "Sometimes it stops after a day or two; other times it pours continuously the whole season. Some years, there was no rain at all, or only a gentle drizzle. Other years, the rain floods the river and makes life difficult." Guru-Ma sipped the warm milk and gestured for Sita to come sit down beside her.

"So tell me dear one," asked Valmiki, "how do you like it here at the hermitage? Who are your friends here and how do you spend your time? And most importantly, what is it like to be Sita these days?"

His gaze was gentle, his voice filled with care and concern for the once- abandoned woman.

Sita felt a lump in her throat as she struggled to find words to express her feelings. Her heart felt an outpouring of emotions ranging from joy for such caring to grief for her lot in life. Somehow, after being rejected by Rama, she had felt broken and unlovable. The kind words of Guru-Ma and Valmiki peeled away the scab that had formed upon her unhealed wounds! It felt as if after a long and hard battle for love, she had just about become reconciled to her fate – that feeling of being unworthy – only to find love being offered to her in unimaginable quantities.

The kind of teary gratitude that an infant feels when she is torn off one breast, simply to be offered the other, came over Sita. If words alone could have expressed all her feelings, there would be no need for silence. But silence filled the room. The eyes of Valmiki and Guru-Ma grew moist with tears as they observed, helplessly, the suffering of their young host.

Sita wept, shedding heavy tears accompanied by loud sobs. With the weeping came a great sense of relief. The fever of her anguish seemed to vanish as Guru-Ma held her hand. Sita felt her closed heart open once again with love.

She whispered words that were punctuated by sobs. "I feel such gratitude towards the two of you for providing me refuge in your hermitage. I cannot understand why I deserve such great kindness. I perhaps invited this cruel fate upon myself, as I feel somehow unworthy and unlovable! Even when I try not to, I feel great anger towards him – my husband and my king – and I wish that he too would suffer. I knew I remained an outsider to the royal family. What else can I feel but hatred towards them! They did nothing to stop my husband from abandoning me. I understand that his brother, Lakshmana, was simply following orders when he left me in the forest, but I am disgusted at his lack of kindness. My own father has done nothing but cry; he pretends his hands are tied by centuries of custom, and I cannot help but feel anger towards his helplessness. Sitting here, right by the two of you who have provided me with shelter and kindness, I feel envy for the love that you both share. Love is all that I have desired my whole life, and now I will never feel it again! Surely I deserve this plight! After all, I am so very flawed that I must be deeply unlovable! When the cruel Ravana captured me and dragged me away to his kingdom, I was defenseless and alone, and all of my pleading for his mercy did nothing to change his resolve. I felt such great disdain for his lack of humanity that I cherished the thought he would die at the hands of my husband. In fact, I felt ecstatic as Rama felled him and experienced strength surging within my bosom as Ravana's head rolled towards my feet. I did not even wince when Ravana shouted out in pain. The whole court and kingdom whispered about the heartless words of a lowly washer-man who refused to take his wife back after she had spent several nights away from him. 'I am not King Rama, to take back a wife who has defiled me by spending a night in another man's home!' he shouted out in the court. Then, I felt confident in Rama's love for me, I felt sure that my high birth and ranking would protect me from such scandal. I felt pity for the wretchedness of those born below me, and contempt for their petty thoughts. But now I see I was wrong, and I loathe myself for my innocent faith in those who could never live up to my expectations. Such great mistrust flows through me that I cannot feel gratitude even towards the two of you without being reminded of my shame. All of this is my own doing. I have earned these grievances because of my arrogance and meanness. I doubt I will even be a good mother to this child. Please show me a way out of this endless misery! Please let me die and take this unwanted child along with me. I deserve nothing else."

Valmiki addressed Sita for the very first time, his voice soft, words flowing slowly, "Tell me, my dear, what do you think will happen to you tonight? Or maybe even tomorrow?"

Sita looked at him quizzically, replying with great hesitation, "I am not sure, revered sage! I do not know what will happen! I'm not sure what you mean."

"Sita, you just told us that you were sure that you will never experience love or happiness ever again in your life! If you cannot predict what is to happen tonight, then how can you be sure of what is likely to happen in the distant future?" Valmiki asked in a steady voice.

"But, I am alone, I have no home or family and I feel sad and miserable often! How then can I foresee love in my future?"

Valmiki smiled benignly. "You are feeling sad and miserable this very moment, Sita! In the next moment you might feel anguish or joy – no one knows! Even I do not know what your future holds for you. All that I wish is for you to become aware of your changing thoughts and emotions. I want for you to be attentive to whichever emotion you may be feeling each moment, Sita. That is all the help I can offer right now."

Noticing that Sita was silent, Valmiki spoke once again, "Be kind to yourself, dear Sita! Try not to judge yourself harshly because of the emotions and thoughts that flit through you. Right now, you have provided such detailed description of your internal life. If only every human would be as alive to his experiences as you have been, my dear, then the world could perhaps become inhabited by a species of enlightened humans. Surely, even kings give birth to humans alone – don't they? Or, am I incorrect in this assumption? You are daughter to the great King Janaka and wife to Emperor Rama, but you too are only human, are you not? Now, who amongst us does not experience anger, ambition, greed or lust, at least occasionally? Was it not the anger of Rama that killed the mighty demon Ravana? Was is not greed for kingship that caused Rama's stepmother to coerce King Dasharatha so that he would send Rama and you into the forest? Was it not grief – and guilt for sentencing Rama to exile – that took the life of the great King Dasharatha? Was it not self-righteousness that caused Rama and the citizens of Ayodhya to abandon you? Even this love between Guru-Ma and I that you imagine to be perfect was threatened by greed this very afternoon, my dear," he added with a smile. "It was threatened by my own greed for her share of the rice pudding that she angrily stopped me from having. I must admit that I too felt a pinch of shame this very afternoon!"

Hearing his last few words, Sita could not repress a quick smile that momentarily brightened her beautiful face.

Guru-Ma laughed – a bubbling sound that filled the small mud hut with a steady stream of happiness. "So, you too are capable of feeling happiness, my dear Sita. Even if it is only for a quick passing second! Think of yourself as the sky, my child. These thoughts and emotions will then seem like clouds that come in and move out. Nothing stays forever! Resisting your feelings can cause great suffering. Invite them all, as and when they may come. Let them stay for as long as they wish to, and they will leave when they are ready. Pay attention to them when they visit you, for they may contain valuable messages to enhance your life and wellbeing. They need to be heard and understood. Is that not what we all wish for my dear, to be heard and to be understood?"

Sita hesitated before she asked, "How does understanding these emotions and thoughts enable me to change my life, Guru-Ma? How do I change these unpleasant circumstances and bring the father of my unborn child to accept me once more?"

Guru-Ma's eyes filled with tears as she replied, "Oh, my dear! You long so very deeply for that man who has rejected you in your hour of need! No, my child! Understanding your thoughts and emotions does not change the path that your life has assumed in any way whatsoever. Unfortunately, we all succumb to destiny, one way or the other! Such understanding allows us only one choice – to choose how we react to the inevitability of our circumstances. You can accept your destiny gracefully and exist with it in peace, or you can fight it and increase your suffering and the suffering of the lives associated with you. The only thing that you can change in this life is yourself and your reaction. You and I have little or no control over anyone or anything else, Sita!"

Sita responded with a quizzical look at Guru-Ma, followed by the question, "If I were to simply observe my thoughts and my emotions without reacting and simply accept that I cannot change anything, would that not bring my life to a standstill, dear Guru-Ma? How would doing anything at all be justified if I were to remain a mere observer?"

Guru-Ma smiled. "Sita, by being aware of your thoughts and emotions, you can be more conscious and less reactive in your choice of action, my dear. Being aware that you are feeling great anger, being aware that you are feeling disgust, being aware that you are thinking that you are unlovable or worthless – all this awareness simply lets you know that the current moment is not the rightful moment for action, for your action is likely to be imprudent and short-sighted driven by the force of your thoughts and emotions. By recognizing them and letting them be, you can control when and how you wish to react and, hopefully, the pause that you take while you recognize them will give you the space to act more consciously and with prudence."

Sita was astonished at the wisdom imparted to her! She felt great curiosity, an eagerness to learn more. "How long does one have to practice such observation before one can be a master, dear Guru-Ma? How long did it take for Valmiki and you to become perfect?" she asked with eager innocence.

"It's a practice, my child, a practice that will have to be followed throughout your life – a practice that enables you to live more peacefully and productively. But as with all practices, you will still face moments of regression and failure. There is no perfection Sita. Perfection is a fabrication of your mind. We are all flawed and imperfect. We are also beautiful and loving." Guru-Ma wore a sweet smile as she said these words.

It was Valmiki's turn to speak. "Be kind to yourself, dear Sita! Have compassion for that woman inside of you who is entrusted with the huge task of bringing this child into the world and caring for it. Have compassion for that woman inside of you who is abandoned by her family and is filled with sadness. Be kind to that woman inside whose dreams of love have been crushed and left to wither. Try to keep in mind that even this woman who has suffered deeply is also capable of experiencing happiness."

While they had been speaking, the rain had gradually slowed to a soft drizzle. Valmiki and Guru-Ma now took her leave, but only after hugging Sita with warm affection. Sita felt strangely relieved. Her spirit felt light. Nothing had changed, she was still alone, and yet she felt protected and cared for. "Self- compassion and kindness." she said aloud. How was it different from self-pity, she wondered.

Her mind raced like that of an addict, her thoughts turning once again to the moment of her abandonment in the forest, and once again she was overcome by anger and deep sadness. But this time she paused to identify her emotions. "I'm feeling sad and I'm feeling angry," she whispered to herself. Once called out by their names, like mischievous children, these emotions fell quiet. Like magic, they shifted. "I'm feeling surprise," Sita whispered in surprise, and a huge smile came upon her face.

Springing up in her was a sudden surge of love for Guru-Ma and Valmiki. "I'm feeling love!" she whispered, even more surprised. Little did she know it had been there. She had been so consumed with her grief that she had never paid attention to all these precious moments that flitted along, sprinkling joy and love, with the sincere hope that their sweet dust would regenerate fresh enthusiasm, once again, for the life in her.

Sita was mesmerized! She was now certain that Guru-Ma and Valmiki knew of a way she could exist peacefully accepting her life and herself. A new desire to know the way was born in her right then! Without being fully aware of what was happening, she was already turning a new chapter in her life. Sita slept peacefully for the rest of the night.

VIII.

QUESTIONS IN THE DARK

Back in Ayodhya, Rama went night after night without sleeping. Near each day's end, as the crimson sunset spilled its inky violet hues in the sky, Rama's heart dreaded the loneliness of his bed-chamber. In the past, the setting of the sun had marked the end of his duties for the day, a time when Rama had been eager to take leave of the administrators and ministers, responding to his heart's longing for the companionship of his wife. There had been ten thousand ways in which their intimacy had been shared. He had secretly relished the sight of her earrings laid absentmindedly upon silk cushions, the smell of her perfume that lingered upon his clothes, her voice that soothed him irrespective of the content of her chatter, the manner in which she twirled her hair when she was nervous, the gentleness with which she rested her head upon his shoulder as they embraced. But now his life felt stripped of beauty. He had banished Sita from his empire and banished meaning from his life.

Rama had known, even as he issued the command to Lakshmana to take Sita to the forest, that his choice would cause him unfathomable grief. What came as a surprise to Rama, was how incensed he felt about the injustice and impropriety of his own righteousness. Regrets devoured him night after night. In the past, he had rarely succumbed to introspection. He had considered himself primarily as a man of action. Internal scrutiny, he had thought, was a hindrance to action, and therefore he had avoided it most of his life. But now it felt as if impulse and action – which once had been one and the same – were as separate as horse and rider. With this distinction between thought and action came relentless soul-searching.

There was no escape in the darkness of silent nights. Drowned thoughts returned like dead and decomposed bodies emerging from deep lakes. Like a mirror reflecting clear light, darkness showed the heart its hidden truths. There was no deliverance, and the alternative of surrender felt unbearable! In the depth of the darkness, his egotistical reasoning lost its valor while naked truth mocked his life and everything it stood for. He, the great emperor, Rama, simply lacked the leadership required to guide his citizens towards what was indeed right, though unpopular and regarded with disfavor. Many a time, his hypocrisy caused despair; in anguish he desired to throw away this mockery of a life studded with values that brought him no peace. His troubled mind panicked, and in its panic concocted reasons – blame, justification, and consolation. He hoped the higher causes he represented would somehow justify his senseless behavior and hide its shame. But the voice that began speaking to him at nightfall was clear. Transparent, now, was the folly of all his unexamined values. His ideology stood empty and hollowed-out before him.

Rama's mighty empire had resonated with the taunting words of a common washer-man, a low-ranking citizen of Ayodhya, an ignorant illiterate; a crude and unsympathetic man.

"I am not the man who will accept a wife who has spent several nights away from my home in the company of another man. Even if our King Rama himself chooses to do so – and brings shame upon this great land," he had said.

Upon hearing these words, the court and the kingdom had demanded answers from their King. Like grieving, insane pilgrims who trash their God and trample him when their prayers go unanswered, they demanded to be shown the full wrath of his power.

His beloved Sita! She was an extraordinary woman. Beautiful, charming, intelligent and caring, she had worked her way into his heart with immense patience. Filled with pride, unable to accept his blooming love for her as a newlywed, Rama had instead worn his pretenses and shielded his love from the sight of others. But she had remained transparent in her love for him from the very start of their married life, confessing it often, displaying it even more frequently, inviting him to feel the deliciousness of the emotion, surprising him, mesmerizing him, enabling him to know the difference between what is manly and what is human. She had carved pathways that enabled him to explore himself in ways he had never done before.

Influenced by his stepmother who wanted her own son, Prince Bharatha, to become the crown prince, Rama's father King Dasharatha had exiled prince Rama to the forest for fourteen years. Rama had not resisted the decision of his father; he had simply obeyed. Then, too, Sita had stood by his side. Giving up all the comforts of the palace, she had followed him to the forest. She had made a home out of the hut that he built for her and comforted his aching heart with her tender companionship and generous kindness.

With all their princely privileges peeled away, their time in the forest enabled them to discover each other's strengths – strengths that were tested to the limits – and to face each other's follies as they emerged into the open. In this new life of theirs, Sita leaned against him with infinite trust and faith that he would bring her nothing but good. Rama, who had no desire to take away her God from her, guarded her young soul with an abandoned display of love and affection. Happiness that seemed hard to come by in the royal parlor was easily accessible here, like the air that one breathes or like cool waters that are swallowed. Life was simply wonderful and surprisingly uncomplicated.

If only! If only he had not desired so very deeply to give her everything that she wished for, then perhaps he would not have been out hunting for the golden deer on the day that the evil Ravana had presented himself before their hut in the forest. How banal was this demon's act of coveting a helpless woman and forcing her into his chariot? In the garb of a hermit, Ravana had come begging for alms and, finding Sita alone, had snatched her away as easily as one plucks fruit from a tree.

How Rama's blood curdled as he imagined Ravana's coarse hands upon Sita's body. The helplessness that Rama felt was intolerable! His grief, immeasurable! Even he, Prince Rama, with all his power, all his strength, all of his heart's blood and all his raging could not protect her. Life lost its appeal. The only thing that kept him alive was his need to be reunited with Sita somehow.

Driven by this need to find Sita once again, Rama had put together an army, a brigade of warriors who though inexperienced, were brave, loyal, and energetic. This army he had led to Lanka, the abode of Ravana, where Sita was being kept captive. A mighty battle ensued between the forces of Ravana and the ragtag army that Rama led. Rama had effortlessly defeated Ravana and severed the demon's head off his body.

As Rama recalled the great battle, he felt his thirst for revenge had gone unquenched even though he had killed the beast! Ravana, even in death, had managed to keep Sita away from Rama by inflaming these rumors. It seemed as if Ravana's shame-filled, beastly act took on a life of its own, outlasting both the victim and the perpetrator.

The dark shaded circles surrounding Rama's eyes were visible evidence of his unspeakable grief. He leaned against his bedpost as he sighed. Why was there no satisfaction in revenge? Why was there no satisfaction in assuming the path of righteous living? Why was it that he, the greatest of great Emperors, could not find re-quiescence in his decisions and contentment within his life?

Rama's mind travelled back to the time when he had seen Sita in the palace gardens of the wretched Ravana. Ah, the pain that his heart felt when he had encountered her for the first time after her ordeal! His beautiful Sita seemed robbed of life. She had closed her eyes and turned her face away from Rama, fearful of contaminating his radiance. Her humiliating captivity had made her feel unworthy of his love. Her helplessness was soaked with shame. A deep shame was branded upon her soul, its venom seeping into Rama's tender heart. Ah, the irony! The shameful act was that of the demon that had been blind to the consequence of his ill will!

Rama's anger flared once again at the thought of Ravana – an unsympathetic animal of a man! So who was this man, with his lust-filled impulsiveness? Was he animal, man, or truly a demon? Rama wondered which God, in what moment of disdainful anguish, had chosen to create this vermin born to desecrate everything that others held sacred!

Rama closed his eyes as hot tears streamed down his cheeks. He imagined his beloved's suffering as captive of Ravana and her seemingly endless suffering since then. He wept loudly as he acknowledged that her continued suffering was a result of his powerlessness over his own citizens! There had been a time in his youth when night was night and day was day, when what was right stood apart from what was wrong. But nothing seemed clear any longer! His life seemed to have turned into a haze through which he stumbled, directionless and lost.

Yet, unknown to Rama, the universe seemed to travel upon its own trajectory without any precognition about the direction of its course. The invisible weighing scales were perpetually balancing out the unequal. What one lacked was balanced by the over-compensation of another. When one person slacked off, another worked harder' when one persisted on living in disgrace, another tempered the universe with soothing calm. Everything in the universe was somehow interlinked; it always had been and would always be so.

It was indeed a pity that sweet, innocent Sita had to bear the brunt of the Ravana's legacy. Rama's slaying of the demon had assuaged his rage. But even if Ravana had lived on, he could not have taken back his deed, which had assumed a life of its own – formless yet potent – altering the course of life and destinies of people who were yet to hear of its existence. Rama felt as if the evil in Ravana's act had been released like raw energy into the world. It seemed as if that evil would have to play itself out, cutting through and caressing many lives before it sputtered out and was assimilated into the whole once again. There was simply no justification for the repercussions caused by evil. There was no way to understand it, nor begin to connect the dots that could link one evil act to the next. Senseless suffering seemed to be its only outcome.

Growing weary of pacing up and down his chamber, Rama went out on his balcony. Resting his hands upon the waist-high balcony wall, he leaned forward, feeling the crisp night air. In the cloudless sky, stars glittered and shone, indifferent to the musings of the emperor of the Earth. The sound of water in the nearby fountains echoed in the dark garden.

Following the scent of jasmine, Rama's gaze drifted toward the delicate vine clinging to the wall. Once again his thoughts were filled with Sita as he reminisced about their lovemaking after he fought the gruesome battle in Lanka to recover her.

In Lanka, while funeral fires burned and bodies, prepared for last rites lined the streets, Rama had gently gathered Sita into his arms, each and every piece of her. He had kissed her gently, whispering his love for her over and over again. They had made love, a fierce kind of love, in which she drew him closer and closer into her as if she wished for her body to melt into his and for her soul to remain his forever. They had stayed together as such for a long, long, time. His touch, Sita claimed, undid the pervasive pollution of the demon, and little by little she had once again come back into being the woman she once was. The pain and delight they experienced in each other's loving arms had been so very wonderful.

And yet Rama's heart had bled with remorse when he visited the battlefield and the city of Lanka shortly after! It was then Rama understood that when a King commits a crime, it's a crime against the whole nation. The people of Lanka, ruled by the demon Ravana, had suffered immensely in the battle. Life had been interrupted, homes burnt, bodies strewn all over. Where blood had flowed in the streets, women and children wailed for the dead. The battlefield was riddled with limbs torn apart, heads severed, bodies sliced by sharp blades. Arrows peeked out of gruesome flesh, and a thick stench of decay filled the air, inviting the circling vultures to swoop down and have their pick. It was then, standing in the blood-drenched battlefield, that Rama had for the very first time questioned its justification. That many lives sacrificed, that many families mourning for the dead, those many orphans all for the sake of one woman! Were his happiness and his love worth the sacrifice of these many?

Ever since that moment, Rama's mind had rankled with doubt! Was it right to sacrifice these many lives to protect one? Was it right to allow one to suffer so that the majority could be peaceful? What was the truth? Why was it that the truth felt two-faced? Rama was deeply troubled.

If there was any other man in existence who loved his wife as Rama loved Sita, he might have provided Rama with the answers he needed! If there had been a man who understood that not even a King could control his destiny, perhaps he would have shared with Rama his wisdom! If only there was a teacher who could bring to light how evil begot evil and explain how we are all participants in its liquid fury – that we bend and sway under its power, satiating it until it suffocates itself with the overwhelming lives that it swallows – then, perhaps, Prince Rama could understand that it was not his desire for happiness and love that had caused the carnage in Lanka but the evil deed of Ravana which had assumed a life of its own!

But the unanswered question of worthiness lingered in Rama's heart, pressing for a resolution that he could not provide. This was the place he had revisited when he directed Lakshmana to take Sita to the forest. This time, Rama justified his sacrifice of Sita just so that the people of Ayodhya would not suffer.

As Rama tossed and turned in bed, birds started to chirp. Finally, he opened his tired eyes to perceive the streak of orange that caressed the eastern sky. Another bold day was on its way, even as he longed to stay inconspicuous and forgotten. In the distance, temple priests sounded conch shells and rang bells to wake up the sleeping Gods. Rama's shoulders felt the burden of centuries-old customs.

How innocently he had assumed their return to Ayodhya would help them put all of the happenings in Lanka behind them. Along with the battle, the fourteen years of exile that his father the late King Dasharatha had imposed on him had ended. The citizens of Ayodhya, he was told, eagerly awaited the return of their prince. He had hoped that Sita and he would find the time to recover and once more forge a brand new life together.

But the thick mantle of centuries of heritage lay heavily on him. In Ayodhya, he was no longer just Rama Sita's beloved husband; here, he was King ruling over the known world. This kingship that he was entitled to as the first-born male child of the great king Dasharatha, this kingship which was his destiny, this kingship that had taken years of concentrated grooming in the arts of warfare and learning, this kingship that his devoted parents had anticipated his ascension to, this kingship that provided him power, wealth and undying loyalty of his people, this kingship which made secure a vast empire and enabled peaceful living for all of its citizens – alas, it was this kingship that would take his beloved from him forever.

From as far back as he could remember, he had always been loved – loved by his father, his brothers, his countrymen, even by his enemies (if out of envy alone). This resentment in the hearts of his countrymen towards Rama, all on account of his queen, made him uneasy and restless.

The carnage at Lanka, the kingdom of Ravana and its still-suffering citizens brought aching to his tender loving heart. The harsh words of the washer-man, taunting him for taking back a dishonored woman as his wife and queen, had raised the question of Rama's righteousness. His ability to rule the kingdom with justice and fairness had come under serious scrutiny. While Rama had felt incapable of quelling these repeated rumors, his heart hurt as people made demands that he dismiss his beloved from the kingdom.

All that Rama experienced in that moment was confusion. Centuries of custom clashed with the wishes of his gentle heart. The thick voice of heritage muted his simple desire for happiness; the path of his ancestors deviated at the point where Rama stood with his hands clasped firmly against Sita's. What was he to do?

In utter confusion, Rama lost all perspective. Like men before him, he had relied on the strength of centuries of custom and of age-old tradition, following the path of the ancestors as he sought answers. In his anxiety the thick walls of institution, hemmed him in even more tightly. His mind hovered over his heart and closed all gateways that would have been considered bold and new.

After all, what is familiar has always been comforting even if the fruits that can be found along a new pathway are more delicious. There are few amongst us who are willing to forsake what is safe in exchange for what is true. Perhaps he was simply fatigued and had no more fight left in him. Anyhow, he ordered his brother Lakshmana, to take his pregnant wife Sita and abandon her in the forest, thereby selecting the way of the familiar and aligning himself with the ordinary. By choosing to forsake his innocent wife, he had forsaken women all over for centuries to come.

IX.

DISCOURSE

Azure morning clouds parted to reveal the bright orange sun reddening the walls of the little hut where Sita slept. She woke up smiling. This morning she was too excited to pay attention to the light that seeped through cracks in the windows making interesting patterns on the cool, hard earth of the floor. She was too excited to pay attention to the lingering fragrance of lavender oil that she applied behind her ears. She was much too excited to taste fully the cooked meal of rice and lentils that was garnished with fresh cilantro. She barely noticed how, even in her pale yellow cotton sari, her dark skin shone radiantly.

She brushed her thick hair and braided it quickly. Today was the day of the discourse! Everyone who was anyone in the hermitage was invited to take part in this ceremony of learning. Sita was eager to participate and learn.

This morning was different for another reason as well! This morning her thoughts had not strayed far into the beyond but had stayed with her, within her tiny hut. Her past was still present within the recesses of her heart but its pain did not torment her. Slowly, her aches and disappointments had begun to recede. Sita was beginning to drift unconsciously into a brand-new sense of what felt everyday and normal. The hope of seeing Rama once again had disappeared altogether. Her emphasis, now, was on the physical, emotional and spiritual wellbeing evoked by the preceptors and other teachers in the hermitage, along with the anticipation of giving birth soon. All this enabled Sita to take a step forward towards a destiny that was completely her own.

As she hurried outside, she paused to remind herself of the child within her belly that was due to be born at any moment. It had been nearly four months since she had arrived at the hermitage, and her pregnancy was full term. She slowed her pace to accommodate her body, smiling brightly as she heaved a breath charged with relief and excitement!

She quickly joined a party of women headed towards the home of Valmiki and Guru-Ma, where the discourse was to be held. She noticed her own joy as she extended and received greetings from all well-wishers.

On entering the premises of their humble home, Sita was struck by its simplicity and elegant beauty. The scent of flowerbeds and growing herbs warmed the morning air and calmed her senses as she walked inside their home. A simple pattern of creepers and flowers, all red and white, decorated the edges of their mud-caked floor. Straw mats dyed bright colors were laid out for the guests to sit upon, and the smell of milk boiled with cardamom and honey wafted from the kitchen. A young girl, her hair in a tight braid decked with fresh flowers and earthy red attire, sat cross-legged upon the floor and skillfully played a slow rhythmic tune on the veena. Plucking the strings with one hand, she moved the other to create notes with such precision that a tremor passed through Sita's body and happiness flooded her heart. Sita brought her hands together to convey her regards to everyone present and took a seat upon the floor.

Silence fell over the room as Valmiki and Guru-Ma entered. Valmiki's eyes drifted over the people in the room as he strode in, stopping at intervals to acknowledge a few familiar faces. His own face filled with delight and surprise when he noted Sita in the room.

Speaking in a soft, clear voice, he said, "We are all seeking answers here. The process of learning is never complete. Let us hope that we will leave today with a sense of having learnt something new. As usual, we will start with a simple incantation. I will describe its meaning to the group, after which I will open up the discussion to questions or observations that any of you may have. At the end of each round of discussion, we will return to share a few moments of silent meditation. This discussion is a way of calming the heart; it is not designed to fulfill the ego. While you meditate, I request that you please be aware of your internal landscape, noticing your thoughts, your emotions, and the sensations within your body. Sometimes, the ego clamoring for attention can highjack a worthwhile discussion, so I request that you be aware of your internal workings." Valmiki and Guru-Ma welcomed their guests with folded hands and sat amongst them in a huge circle. The discourse was started with the incantation:

ॐ पूरणमदः पूरणमिदं पूरणात् पूरणमुदच्यते ।
पूरणस्य पूरणमादाय पूरणमेवावशिष्यते ॥
ॐ शान्तिः शान्तिः शान्तिः॥

Aum pūrnamada pūrnamidam pūrnāt pūrnamudacyate |
pūrnasya pūrnamādāya pūrnamevāvaśishyate ||
Aum śāntih śāntih śāntih ||

Valmiki explained:

"This incantation describes the primary source of all life. The primary source is described as something that is complete in itself, full and without an end like a circle. Everything that exists in creation comes from within this primary source and, like the source everything in creation is also complete, full, and without an end. The primary source precedes everything that comes from it and continues to remain complete, full, and endless despite manifesting itself in several forms and creations. May there be peace! May there be peace! May there be peace!"

"The first incantation for peace is from the suffering that we experience as a result of conflicts within ourselves from time to time. The second incantation for peace is from the suffering that we experience, as we perceive our self as something that is different and unique from those around us. The third incantation for peace is from the suffering we experience as we feel the separation from our primary parent. This felt separation from the parent causes the feeling of being orphaned and all alone in the world. Once we experience unity with everything around us within our body, and not just in our thinking minds, the ego-driven identity disappears and suffering ceases."

"Now," concluded Valmiki, "I open the discussion to questions and encourage everyone in here to share your observations."

The bright and inquisitive eyes of Sanathana, a new disciple of Valmiki's, lit up with delight as the discussion opened. He was dressed in white garments with his hair pulled behind his head in a tuft, wearing on his wrist dark brown rudraksha beads that almost blended in with the color of his skin. Young, curious, and eager to learn, he posed the first question: "Does that mean the divine parent exists in everything and that everything is divinity? Is this limited to living things alone, or are things that appear not to be living also a part of the divine parent?"

Valmiki answered, "If you were to fill a container with water from the river, the contents of the container would still be water and the river would still be full. Similarly, everything in creation is composed of the primary source of life, and this composition is not taking away anything from the parent who continues to remain intact. And which are those things that we consider to not possess life? Does the wind not erode the mountains and change its appearance? Does flowing water not smooth the surface of river stones? Does a piece of wood not disintegrate into the soil? Everything in and around us is changing and alive in ways unique to its own self. So, in my mind it would be right to assume that everything is composed of the same life that is shared with the primary parent."

Sanathana nodded in understanding. His striking features shone with radiance as he closed his eyes and inhaled luxuriously! Following the lead of Guru-Ma and Valmiki, the group returned to silent meditation. Sitting upright with their eyes gently closed, they traced their breath, simply observing each inhalation and exhalation.

Then Guru-Ma intervened. "If you find your mind drifting, please bring your mind back to observing the breath with kindness and without judgment. If your body is immersed in the feeling tone of an emotion, observe the quality of the emotion and return to following your breath with care. Please feel free to adjust your posture, should you be in discomfort, and pay attention to the sensations within your body as you once again come back to observing your breath."

After a few more moments, the group returned once again to the discussion.

Govinda, a seasoned disciple – short and stocky in stature – was seated beside Valmiki in the group. Having come into the hermitage at a very early age, he had chosen to remain there for a number of years. An all-too-familiar figure, he was entrusted with the task of caring for the cattle within the hermitage. With his hand raised to his chin, he posed the next question with a bit of hesitation. "If the primary source does manifest itself in several forms, then does the primary source need the support of such manifestations in order to exist? In other words, do we define the primary source just as much as the primary source is what defines our existence?"

Valmiki smiled as he answered, "I cannot satisfactorily answer your question, Govinda! I can only tell you that thought and thinking is only one of the ways of conscious existence, and knowing cannot be through the intellect alone. Having these thoughts for which we cannot find satisfying answers is a form of suffering in itself! If any of you have an opinion that is otherwise, I welcome you to share it with the rest of the group. I will add that 'life' does not start or end with 'human' life alone! Therefore I consider it only an assumption of ours that the primary source resembles us humans or that we play a special role in existence."

Atreya, a quiet disciple, indicated his desire to speak before the group. After Valmiki nodded his head in consent, Atreya spoke in a soft yet clear voice. "I may not be able to answer this question either, as I simply cannot affirm nor can I deny the possibility of the primary source needing us just as much as we need it. All that I wish to say is that when we experience our self as something that is different from the whole, it causes us deep suffering, as we feel all alone and orphaned as a result of such separation. But when our hearts are filled with love and compassion for all creatures around us, our suffering diminishes. I therefore assume that the way to find peace within our questioning minds is to approach the questions themselves with deep compassion."

With this, the group of participants once again returned to the practice of meditation in silence. Sita felt a deep sense of fulfillment and peace within her body. Sitting here amidst sages and scholars, she felt at home. She noticed how she experienced a sense of kinship with these men and women. She noted with surprise that in this moment she was no longer bitter about the rejection she had experienced not so long ago! Her presumed loss, she realized, was perhaps not a misfortune after all! The child within her had calmed down and seemed curiously absorbed in this peaceful ritual as well.

Sita, hesitatingly, asked the next question. "Are people who are angry and filled with hatred a part of the divine, too? If we are all the same, then why is it that we even feel dislike and hatred towards another? Are these parts of our own self that we hold in spite?"

Guru-Ma responded after careful consideration, "Emotions move in and out of us in the same manner as clouds move in the sky. People who are angry, who harbor hatred, and those who are disrespectful of life are also manifestations of the divine parent. And the felt anger, hatred or dislike, is nothing but a fleeting emotion. We cannot judge the universal parent by the quality of the mind that it is enmeshed with, just as we cannot judge our own self by the strength of a fleeting emotion. Emotions, too, like thoughts and sensations, are only a part of inner consciousness. But neither one of those emotions, nor all of them put together, make our consciousness whole. Since we can observe our thoughts and we can observe our emotions, the observer, which is the consciousness, has to be different from the thoughts we think or the emotions that we feel. It seems to me that nothing in nature is redundant. Our emotions, too, have a purpose in the grand scheme of life. Anger, envy, greed, lust, and hate also have as much purpose as love, joy, gratitude, and compassion. None of us can avoid these emotions, not even the so-called enlightened ones.

"Regarding your question about whether these seemingly hard emotions like anger, hatred and disgust mean that we are unconsciously directing this towards our self – I can only tell you, dear Sita, to try and not judge nor push away whatever it is that you are feeling. Simply acknowledge it and let it be."

Hearing these words from Guru-Ma brought a sense of relief to the group. Valmiki smiled at his wife, feeling deep gratitude for her presence in his life. Sita's eyes moistened, as she felt accepted for the very first time in her life, just as she was, with her faults and strengths alike.

Valmiki looked intently at Sita as he spoke. "However, recognizing the universality of life should not be used as an excuse to tolerate hurtful behavior Sita! When people cause you pain, you are responsible for protecting yourself! You can draw in your boundaries and keep away those that cause you suffering. But in doing so, act with kindness and not with anger. Wish that the person who causes you pain, be free of suffering, wish them happiness, and wish that they find a way to live peacefully. But first be kind to the person within you who suffers and offer your compassion to that person, too."

The group then returned to the practice of meditation for a few more moments in absolute silence. Tears streamed down Sita's face as she heard the kind words of Valmiki and Guru-Ma. Her body relaxed and her breath eased into peace-filled comfort.

Lalitha, a kind and generous woman who had suffered grievously in her life, asked the next question, "What actions would be right and what would be wrong if people are made of the same element as the divine? Would it not be so that we are judging the divine parent when we judge a murderer?"

Valmiki replied with kindness, "In the absolute sense, there is no right-doing or wrong-doing. But know in your heart that the ocean feeds the clouds, which in turn feed the rivers that flow back to the ocean. All of life is interdependent, and so are we humans. Therefore, working towards the collective wellbeing of all is the indication of a cultivated and responsible mind, and working for the satisfaction of oneself is the working of a mind that is conceited. Caring and compassion are ingrained within the human soul; if that were not so, then the world would be filled with murderers. When we judge a murderer, we are judging the mind of a murderer that has deviated from the collective objective of a peaceful universe. There is the element of the divine in the murderer as well! We should try to keep those who hurt us close to our hearts, and yet we can choose to keep them out of our life. "

He paused for a bit before continuing.

"Individual well-being changes with the passage of time. By honoring the well being of individuals, we also honor the well being of the collective. Even ancestral customs and age-old traditions have to be revisited time and again to reflect the needs of the individual. For the entire group can function as a tyrant against an individual at times. In my mind, it is not appropriate to masquerade in the garments of a bygone era simply because people are reluctant to change. Well-being is a balance of individual and collective needs. And when in doubt it is always best to listen to the voice within and proceed with great wisdom and patience. "

Inquisitive Lalitha, not entirely satisfied by Valmiki's response persisted, "Would introspection and awareness of our internal workings ensure that the path assumed is the right one?"

Valmiki inhaled deeply and closed his eyes for a moment. He felt the anxiety experienced by the troubled woman and the confusion that prevailed in her mind. He smiled at Lalitha as he opened his eyes once more and spoke with great caring and compassion, "I can only hope that the path assumed will be the right one. With introspection – and by pausing to observe the forces within us that are provoking action – we can prevent deeds resulting from an unstable mind. Hopefully the pain of our suffering will open our hearts to far greater understanding. It is important to cultivate compassion and kindness both towards others and towards the self."

The group returned to the practice of meditation once more. Outside, a gentle breeze had picked up, rustling a few dried leaves. The barking of a dog could be heard in the distance along with the high-pitched voices of children at play. The words 'compassion for self' had been uttered once again, and Sita's curiosity was piqued. She noticed her own impatience as she waited for the practice to end just so could ask the next question. She wondered what the difference was between self-compassion and self-pity.

Lalitha spoke once again, as if anticipating Sita's question. "Guru-Ma, how is self compassion different from self-pity?"

Guru-Ma replied in a gentle voice, "When you are in deep pain you are more likely to grasp at something that would heal you than one that can hurt you even more – is that not so? The difference between these two emotions may seem subtle, but their influence is significant. When Valmiki left me, I felt great anger and resentment towards him, and I constantly wallowed in self-pity. I cried, hungering for his return, and experienced great fear for the well being of the children. This made me feel even more helpless and angry, and so I felt greater pity for myself. None of this changed my situation, of course! One day, out of sheer anger and helplessness, I hit my son who cried because he was hungry. My heart was filled with hatred; ignoring him, I hurried to the well to get water. When I looked into the well, I saw my reflection and I could not recognize myself anymore. In all the years of my life, everyone around me had cherished me for my bright, smiling face. Yet in my reflection, I saw a woman with dark moons underneath her eyes, a forehead filled with lines of worry, and a mouth twisted in anger. Who was she, that woman in my reflection? I wondered. I turned my attention towards her life. I watched her as she tried as hard as she could to do the best by her children. I watched her working day and night to simply get by. I watched how she had no time to care about her appearance. I felt a wave of compassion come within me for that woman who was none other than myself. I cried once again, for all of the suffering that had befallen me. When I was done crying, I looked intently at my reflection. This time, I could see a woman who felt understood. Her face was soft and she looked relieved. In an instant, I found myself laughing at my life. Laughing at the hopes of the young bride who had married Valmiki, trusting that he would do her nothing but good, laughing at my husband who had gone away to find his peace, and laughing at the grieved and angry woman I had become. That laughter, driven by compassion, made me realize that I was taking all my fears and assumptions a bit too seriously. It had been three whole months since Valmiki had left us, yet here I was! Life was difficult, for sure. But I was alive and was loved by my children. I hurried back home to console my young son and feel his little arms around my neck."

"That's the difference! With self compassion I could heal myself but with self pity I just plunged deeper into my sorrow!"

Valmiki's eyes had remained closed as he listened attentively to Guru-Ma's words. When he opened them, Guru-Ma saw that his eyes were moist. She met his gaze with kindness.

"The moment is gone, Valmiki! It's an old story whose characters are long dead!" she whispered.

He smiled gently, his gaze filled with love and compassion. The group had fallen silent. Each felt the affection that existed between the couple. It felt as if the air was tinged with the essence of love and well-being and everyone experienced a sense of gratitude.

The group returned to the practice once again. With closed eyes, Sita explored her internal life. She was still and quiet like a peaceful lake, reflecting the sky and surroundings like in a mirror, yet aware that a lake is composed of water alone. Sita's mind and body were both relaxed, and now the life within her belly turned around and kicked violently as if craving attention. Sita felt the very first contraction and winced slightly. Many in the group were startled!

Within seconds, Sita's body shook with another contraction. Guru-Ma, patiently, without panic, asked for the men in the group to take their leave. She then ordered Lalitha to gather some others to provide assistance. Sita felt the nervous energy of fear and excitement!

Soon, Sita would become a mother!

X.

TWINS

Sita was in labor.

Guru-Ma directed the women to move her into the inner chamber of their small home. Sita clutched the bare wooden doorpost, winced, then shuddered as a raw ache gripped her lower back and abdomen and squeezed her body. She buried her fingers into Lalitha's shoulder as the pain increased exponentially, then subsided. Pausing to catch a full breath once again, Sita offered an apology to the smiling young woman.

Sita was led into a tidy room with white walls. A bed with a thin cotton mattress stood in the center of the room. Thinly woven jute shades covered the windows, creating patterns of light and shadow on the cool, mud-caked floors. The room smelled of camphor and flowers. Sita peeked through one of the open windows to observe a carefully laid-out garden surrounding a red and white clay pot holding the sacred herb tulsi. A piece of lit camphor had been placed before the tulsi, and decorative white chalk patterns marked the earth around the clay pot.

Lalitha helped Sita settle down upon the mattress and arranged an assortment of pillows against her back to make her comfortable. Two other women brought in a large copper basin filled with hot, steaming water. Guru-Ma rushed behind them, her hand filled with fresh clean towels.

Suddenly, panic gripped Sita, as the contractions got steadier and faster. The women reassured her gently, maintaining their calm as they whispered soft words of encouragement. Sita leaned into their support and followed all of their directions as best she could. She stayed focused on her breath, taking sips of water in between contractions. Holding Guru-Ma's hand tightly, Sita felt her own hand clasped firmly in return.

Outside, cloudy evening blues swallowed the late afternoon sky. The wind blew carelessly across the terrain; restless and uncertain, it seemed to arise mysteriously, as if stirring a strange desire to name new Gods, write new prayers, and pay diligence. Valmiki sat outside his home, offering prayers to whichever God would hear them, to help young Sita live through her new ordeal.

The women around Sita wiped her eyebrows and damp forehead. They rubbed her cold feet between the palms of their hands and gently massaged her aching back. The violence of the pains that rocked her body filled Sita with a vague, exciting fear. No longer able to hide her vulnerability in the grip of this steadily increasing torment, she finally gave into it completely, screaming aloud when she felt the pain to be unbearable. Intermittently, whenever her body allowed her to divert her attention, Sita felt immense gratitude for the presence and care of these women. She found herself drawing strength from their support as if they were family: the distinction had disappeared, the boundaries faded. The women kept her informed of her progress, praising her for every bit of her effort.

Soon, the dark nighttime clouds set in and a steady drizzle filled the air. In the flickering lights of oil lamps that lit the room, the rain resembled a million flecks of light descending from the heavens. The winds calmed and finally crept away into the darkness of the woods. Now the baby's head had crowned and the baby was ready to tear away. When Sita pushed, the baby co-operated. Like a well-practiced orchestra, they both performed what was required of them involuntarily with great expertise.

And then he emerged – a screaming mass of precious life waving his arms and kicking his feet at everyone. Strong and healthy, he filled his lungs and announced his arrival with a war cry demanding the care of his mother. Sita wept when she saw his little pink fingers and his tiny nose, feeling a surge of love like none she had never experienced flooding her body as she gently touched the baby. She had almost forgotten the extended ordeal she had undergone in producing him when, suddenly, those scorching contractions resumed once again.

Another well kept secret would be revealed; with a momentary force that was filled with emotion. The women, surprised and alarmed, rushed back into position to assist as they realized another newcomer was on the way! With determination and speed, he was ready to make haste and claim his mother all to himself, now that his brother was out. And just like that, he came – another beautiful, healthy baby boy who wouldn't stop crying until he was reunited with his brother now resting safely on their mother's bosom.

Sita's happiness knew no bounds. She cried joyous tears and kissed both of her children. The miracle had been performed once again – the miracle that happens every single day and yet retains its claim as the most intriguing one of all – the miracle of life!

The newborn babies, cleaned and wrapped in warm blankets, were placed on Sita's breasts. They ate eagerly, hungrily, and then slept peacefully on her warm, bare skin as if knowing they would be safe forever. Radiant warmth swept over Sita as she held these brand new sprigs of life against her full breasts. She felt the longing to live once again, to live for them, to live with them, and live joyously! She pledged silent allegiance to them, swearing to protect them from everyone and everything, including herself. Now that they had come to her, she was determined to have the world move around and make way for them, even if she was single-handed and frail. Sita fell into a sleep that wiped away the exhaustion of labor until all that remained was like a memory of a forgotten dream. The three of them were knit into a harmony that could not be touched by the world outside.

Guru-Ma stepped outside to announce the births to Valmiki, whose grandfatherly face was filled with eager curiosity. He smiled graciously at the news, and warm tears of gratitude filled his narrow, crinkled eyes. Yet, sadness descended upon him; as he thought of Rama and his loss at not being able to hold these precious ones against his chest and feel the irrefutable continuity of his life. Valmiki wept tears at the foolishness of mankind that seemed to be forever chasing after immortality as if it were something that was out there and possible to acquire! This was the only way in which it was possible – giving birth to these brand new vessels of life that mocked wildly at the insult of death granted to us by the Gods.

At the insistence of Valmiki and Guru-Ma, Sita stayed in their home for a few more days after giving birth to her twin sons. Motherhood wiped her slate clean and redefined her role and purpose in life. A meaningful direction, a forceful determination, strength like none other and an indomitable love had seized her heart. She forgot her own self and all her pain in the presence of her babies. The demands of caring for them were simply delicious. Their cries were like music to her shunned soul as their delicate fingers brushed her hair and the touch of their skin healed the pain within her heart. Merely by their presence, they drew her into the strong bonds of a family that would always belong to her – and where she would always belong. A warm reassurance filled her heart and chased away all fears. She resolved to carve a new path for herself and her two children. It was as if she felt her destiny in her very bones. There was no time to stop or ponder now; the definitive moment for her to redefine her life had arrived.

Soon eleven days had passed. The babies, well nursed and nourished, thrived. The time had arrived to give them suitable names. It was customary to call in priests and astrologers to mark out the position of the planets at the time of birth in order to predict the destinies of the newly born and give them names that would reflect their fathers and forefathers. But where were they? All those forefathers and fathers – were they ready to accept these children? Sita looked into the small and radiant faces of each of the twins as they looked back at her. She realized they were her whole world, and she was theirs. She noted, with a smile on her face, the close resemblance the babies bore to their father – a resemblance that would remind her of Rama for the rest of her life. Yet all she could feel at the moment was divine love and compassion towards them.

All this time, and during the preceding years, Sita had wondered what caused the great King Janaka, her father and ruler of Mithila, to name her Sita, meaning a "Plow". A piece of farm equipment! He had laughed when, as a young child, she had questioned him. Casually, her father said that even he did not fully understand why the high priest had suggested that it was her destiny to be named as she was. That destiny had remained hidden from her. But now she realized what it was! The purpose of Sita, a plow, was to turn the soil of the earth and give it new life – a life whose "moment and means" had come by way of giving birth to her twin sons. She named her first-born Lava, meaning "moment," because he had defined the moment of change within her. The moment of his birth had rekindled the desire to live in her once again. And she named his twin brother Kusha, meaning "the rope that harnesses the plow."

His birth too had enabled her to function in the same manner as a plow could function, only with the support of the rope that harnesses it. He was to enable Sita to plow the soil and give all of earth a brand-new life. If Lava had brought in the right "moment," Kusha had brought in the "means!" The machinery was in place and the instrument was harnessed. Now the moment had arrived to begin the change she was destined to experience!

Sita reluctantly recalled the words of a young servant who had cared for her when she had been abducted by the evil Ravana. A fairly young maid, a woman of great wisdom, had been entrusted to care for Sita while she was held captive in the palatial gardens of her abductor. That maid, dressed in rags, sat quietly beside Sita, waiting patiently for her to be done with all her helpless crying and wailing!

Once Sita was relatively calm, the maid had spoken to her in a deep yet gentle voice: "My dear, I am not literate, nor am I of royalty like you. But, like you, I too am a woman. While I do not approve of Ravana's actions, I am incapable of preventing them either. Take heart, my dear, and do not sully your pure conscience by accepting responsibility for his cruel doings! Remember, no man can ever take from us that which we do not give from our hearts! Even if the monster takes what he assumes is his, you will still remain complete, whole, and full within yourself if only you muster enough courage to respect the woman that you are."

"Surely we all hope that a day will come when men and women can regard each other with respect and kindness! Perhaps today is still not ready for such greatness! Perhaps we women as mothers have to show our sons a path different from that of their fathers and grandfathers! Perhaps our sons, too, require great courage to walk on this un-trodden path and are not fully equipped with the heart to do it! Only a child who has seen his mother as a complete human, as a person who treats herself with respect and kindness, can grow up to be respectful and kind to other women. Your husband King Rama will surely come back for you someday, and you too will be the mother of sons. Then will come your opportunity to transform the earth and create the balance it needs between man and woman."

Back then Sita had been astonished at the wisdom of a common maid. But she was much too angry and grieved to pay heed to those words! All that she desired was for her dear Rama to slice the demonic Ravana into as many bits as he could and have his head roll down to her feet.

She laughed aloud at herself now! Where was her husband, Rama? Where was her father, Janaka? Where were the royal priests and princes? What satisfaction did the death of Ravana provide her? Here she was alone – facing the prospect of parenting her twin sons all by herself! But she felt liberated in her aloneness somehow, as if by letting go of the expectations of various individuals and communities, she had unburdened both herself and them. She could therefore walk upon the earth like she was the very first human.

"Home is only within myself, or not at all," she said aloud and smiled at the sleeping infants.

At the very same time, elsewhere, in the kingdom of Ayodhya, another mother was desperately trying to mend the broken life of her son! Kaushalya, the mother of King Rama, had summoned him to visit her in her palatial home. Deeply concerned that the kingdom would be left without an heir, she wished for King Rama to wed once again and provide that heir. As she sat supervising the servants who were carrying out their chores, she pondered on the choice of her words and rehearsed the tone in which she was to convey the urgency of the situation.

Rama would join her for lunch that very day, and she urged the servants to hurry and prepare all his favorite foods. Her body ached, and all her royal silks and jewelry sat gaudily upon her thin frame. Somehow, a life spent in conforming to the norm and doing what was expected had not brought forth any security from grief or sorrow. As she sat in her huge palatial home alone – deprived of the laughter of young children – she felt hollow and broken inside.

The convoy arrived! King Rama rode in majestically, seated upon his horse. A maid rushed to convey the news of the King's arrival! Kaushalya, smiling brightly, walked courteously towards him. Their relationship had always been practiced and formal. Mother and son briefly held each other and smiled. They exchanged common courtesies discussing their health and well being; then shared random bits of news from around the kingdom. Kaushalya led Rama to the dining hall where the two of them enjoyed lunch as they continued to talk about happenings elsewhere.

After the meal, as they relaxed in the parlor, an awkwardness fell between them! Soon, silence filled the room – the kind that falls between hearts too fearful of exposing their vulnerability to one another.

Kaushalya spoke hesitatingly, "Son, what is done is done and it's time to look ahead. A kingdom needs kings, and kings marry to make kings. But your bed is empty. Choose a new bride and make her your queen and guarantee me successors to this empire," she pleaded.

Rama exhaled and smiled sadly. Before him sat this woman who had given birth to him, raised him and cared for him – and yet she knew nothing of his heart. Perhaps she did not know her own heart! Life had bedecked her with kingdom and duty, and she had willingly surrendered to its necessities, never questioning what was expected from her as queen. Having lived too many years in dedicated compliance, her heart was shut and unfeeling. She only knew what was required of her, nothing beyond, and she knew it was her duty to command her son to produce an heir to the throne.

"I cannot, dear mother! I had sworn to Sita that she would be my one and only queen in this lifetime. I have given my word, and even you know it is the foremost duty of a king to remain true to his word. My brothers have wives and they will have children soon, the lineage will continue, but it is with sadness I note that I will never get to hold close a child of my own."

Having said so he left his mother, heavy at heart and inconsolable. She did not understand this love that he spoke of; she had never tasted it, never explored it, never allowed her self to feel it to the fullness of her bosom. It was too frightening, and it made her feel all exposed and vulnerable. That being so she had guarded her life against it. Now in the depth of sorrow she had nowhere to take refuge. After all, her husband King Dasharatha had picked other Queens and concubines with ease to suit his pleasure. What power did this single girl from Mithila hold over her precious son? Alas! She had robbed him of all his happiness and mesmerized him with her potent love and rendered him weak and useless. As his mother, Kaushalya had tried hard to undo his feelings for Sita, but she had simply failed.

XI.

MOTHERHOOD

Having recovered from childbirth, Sita longed to return to her hut in the hermitage. She thanked Guru-Ma and Valmiki for all the help she had received from them as she told them her desire to return. Tears flowed from Sita's eyes as she embraced Guru-Ma with great warmth!

Guru-Ma accompanied Sita to her hut, situated just a few houses away down the lane – so close that Guru-Ma would not have to travel far should Sita need assistance of any kind.

As they walked slowly, each carrying one of the bundled infants, Guru-Ma gently asked, "Tell me, Sita, how do you feel about caring for your infant sons?"

Sita hesitated a bit before answering, "Guru-Ma, I would be lying if I were to tell you that I am not fearful of caring for my boys all alone. Everything I have out here is because of the generosity of sage Valmiki and you. This home that I pretend is mine is also what has been given to me. But I think I will be most comfortable in a space where I can be alone with my infants. I have to learn to provide for them, Guru-Ma! I want so many things to be done right by them. So I am a bit excited even though I have never cared for infants before."

Guru-Ma nodded and smiled. Young Sita had no idea of the surprise that awaited her.

Even from a distance, Sita heard the singing of women dressed in bright colored saris who had gathered before her front door. Elaborate patterns, engaging to the eye, had been drawn in white chalk powder outside the front door of her humble home. This, Guru-Ma explained to Sita, was to welcome prosperity and joy into her home. Smiling, Sita gazed at the familiar faces before her. One of the more elderly women stepped forward to place a small red vermillion mark on Sita's forehead; this was to strengthen her inner wisdom and concentration. Two other women, bearing a circular copper plate holding a lamp surrounded by vermillion and turmeric filled water, lifted their offering to Sita and the infants. This was done to rid them of the evil eye and all other forms of darkness and to protect the forces of joy entering the household. The women sang songs, wishing the newborn twins great happiness, longevity, wisdom, wealth, and fame in their lives. The sweet smell of freshly cooked food wafted in the air, stirring an appetite in the new mother.

Sita stepped into a clean home. There was a pile of clothing for the newborn, including blankets and washcloths placed in two large baskets set against the walls. Two simple cradles, crafted out of color-filled fabric, hung from hooks attached to the wooden roof beams. The women explained to Sita that they had established a calendar defining their roles in assisting her. Some would be bringing in fresh warm meals, others helping out with her chores and sleeping over at nighttime, to aid her and to enable her to have the time for her own grooming and prayers. The whole community had been mobilized to help raise the twins and assist Sita. She was surprised and delighted at all the support offered; tears of happiness flooded her luminous black eyes as she smiled radiantly.

Once the new mother and her twins were safely situated in their home and were resting, Guru-Ma spoke to the assembled women: "In nature everything has a language that is unique, it merely needs the opportunity to express itself unhindered. The babies will teach the mother everything she needs to know about them, and she will learn to read their needs by instinct alone. Several of us out here are mothers and grandmothers who have a lot of experience with newborn infants. But I ask you to save your advice and provide it only when it is asked for. Please allow the young mother to know and care for her children in her own way, but provide her with all the help she may need. Offer words of encouragement, praise her for a job well done, and exercise patience at times when she will fumble. In moments of temptation, when you desire to point out what you assume you are generously giving her, try and remember what she has had to lose in order to receive your offering. Please remember that she and her sons are a family now, and respect their need to remain as such. I am deeply grateful to each and every one of you for helping out."

The women smiled at Guru-Ma and nodded in agreement.

Mothering came naturally to Sita; she felt as if a raw energy had come alive within her. It filled her with supreme joy and exaltation, making her feel richness and strength. A strong urge to do things right by her children became her central purpose. Over the next few days and weeks, she discovered that she clearly reveled in her role as a mother. Suddenly, many new resources came awake within her – resources she never even knew she possessed until this moment. The loneliness and sorrow of her earlier days at the hermitage had disappeared altogether; the babies simply made life vibrant and pleasantly satisfying.

In caring for the little ones. She found there never seemed to be enough hours as each day came hard on the heels of another. Every time she looked into the beautiful and cheerful faces of her infants, they looked back into her eyes with equal joy. There was something absolutely beautiful in this magnificent love that seemed to fill all three hearts from the same fountain – beauty in the knowledge that this love was real, pure, clear, transparent, innocent, unassuming, demanding, needy, and simply lacking in pretense.

Though the twin boys looked very much alike, they were not identical. Like Sita, the boys had dark-colored skin, and they seemed to have inherited her luxurious smile, bending their lips into lovely bows with gracious curves. But their noses and eyes resembled those of their father. They had inherited from Rama his broad forehead, deep brown reflective eyes, and a nose that even in infancy seemed chiseled and handsome. It was hard to tell them apart at a single glance, but upon closer inspection the differences became obvious. Lava's face was round and wide while Kasha's was a bit longer and oval. Needless to say, they were both gorgeous!

Within months it was apparent that their personalities, too, were different. Lava, the older one, was precocious, keeping Sita and her helpers constantly on their feet. He wailed with a high-pitched cry, as if in anger, if he was not fed the very instant he woke up. During this infantile display of emotion, his face turned red as he tightened his fists and curled his feet, screaming shrilly until Sita offered her breast. Once at her breast, he continued to let out muffled sobs for a few more seconds as though he were thoroughly disappointed in his mother for not having anticipated the exact moment when he needed her.

Kusha, the younger of the two, was much more patient. Happy and content with everything that came his way, he seldom cried and was always smiling at everyone.

Sita assumed her role as mother with great passion. It was as if she were a companion and mother all at once. She established healthy routines of feeding, bathing, and bedtime for the infants, and with the same fervor, formulated routines for singing, story-time, and play. She sang songs as she tickled their bellies; she got lost in the vivid description of the stories she narrated to them even when they could not understand her words. Very often, mostly in the afternoons, the three of them could be seen sitting on the large wooden swing outside their home. It was quite a sight to witness the boys lazing comfortably in their mother's lap or being lovingly cradled in her arms.

Occasionally, and mostly at night when the moon shone brightly in the sky and seeped in like a silver spray through the window touching the floor of her hut, Sita felt much bewilderment at the turn her young life had taken. There were moments when her heart, blessed with love, felt so very open that it seemed to contain within its domain her lingering love for Rama as she had known him – as a devoted husband and a beloved lover. In these moments, she wished he were there with the three of them sharing in this joy that belonged to him as well. Just as the generosity of the given moment enlarged and enveloped her whole heart, her pain and anger erupted.

Sita observed how the happiness of the twins had made her softer and more loving towards all, and yet in moments the very thought of Rama infused her with hot vapors of fury. This made her sad. She wondered if this anger would ever leave her; it seemed like sluggish sour venom that had seeped in and glazed over her heart.

By the end of the first year, the infants had grown into curious toddlers. Guru-Ma paid her customary visit to Sita on the day the infants were a full year old. She brought colorfully painted wooden toys – horses and elephants – along with fresh fruits from the garden and warm blankets she had woven from bright orange and yellow thread.

As always, Sita was delighted to see her patron, and greeted her warmly. Lava and Kusha, who were just then beginning to walk, took a few hasty steps towards Guru-Ma before both seemed to decide at the same moment that it would be much quicker to simply crawl to her. With their brown mesmerizing eyes, tan skin, plump little bodies and soft baldheads; they delighted Guru-Ma, who chased the tumbling toddlers across the room.

After a morning filled with play and fun, the twins settled down for an afternoon nap. Guru-Ma and Sita ate a quick meal of milk and fruit before they turned to the task of separating the husk from the grain. They sat before Sita's home in the warm sunlight, chatting and laughing as they worked.

Once again, Sita thanked Guru-Ma for her kindness and support.

After a moment's hesitation, she said, "Guru-Ma, I have much to be grateful for. My life in the hermitage with my sons has given me far greater riches than that I ever had within the comfort of my palace home. And yet at times my heart is filled with anger towards the people of Ayodhya and King Rama. Will I ever be rid of this anger? It makes me feel unworthy of the love that I have received from everyone here at the hermitage, for I fear that I will be disliked strongly if they ever know the venom within my heart."

Guru-Ma set aside the sieve that she had been holding and looked closely at the young mother. "My dear Sita, when Valmiki left me several years back, I too felt deep anger and hatred towards him. I felt the sting of betrayal each morning when I woke in a house filled with hungry children. It is indeed an injustice to be abandoned by the ones you love the most. As humans, we are dependent on each other and it's natural to feel angry when we are let down. But, my dear, wounds heal even though sometimes they may leave a scar. If this is the season for great happiness with a few hints of anger, then let it be! Just observe your anger and be aware of it, lest it should provoke you into doing things that you will regret.

Once again my child be compassionate to the woman inside of you who has suffered so very greatly. Be kind to yourself, dear Sita!

"Your healing will take a course of its own, my dear. It might bear a resemblance to mine; and while I can get close to your experience, I cannot know it in the same manner you do. We all remain alone in how we experience our lives, dear Sita. We are all alone! Some of us are aware of it while the vast majority of us avoid knowing it because of the discomfort it generates."

A flock of sparrows suddenly descended before them, obviously hoping to glean a late afternoon snack. Sita threw a handful of grain in their direction, and the two women sat quietly watching the birds.

After a few moments, Sita persisted, "Guru-Ma, was it then incorrect for me to have expectations of my husband? If we are all alone, even when we are dependent on each other, then how do we hold ourselves responsible?"

Guru-Ma chuckled softly as she replied, "No, my child, you can have as many expectations from those that you love as you please. There is no limit there. But your expectations are yours alone. Bear in mind that what you expect and what the other person can give may not be one and the same. You have a choice to make at that point, dear Sita. You can choose to love them as they are. Or, close your heart to them because they cannot become that which you wish for them to be. The only person you can change in this world is your own self!"

Guru-Ma stretched out her legs and leaned against the outer wall of Sita's hut before she continued, "You may have had the expectation that Rama will love and protect you always. Obviously he has failed you! No matter whom you convince of your right doing and his wrongdoing bear in mind that such convincing does not change your situation. Are you now being responsible for your own peace and well being? Where is this thought process taking you?"

Sita looked disappointed. She scanned her surroundings as if searching for the right words to say, then decided to question Guru-Ma once again.

"But Guru-Ma, there is no defined path for a woman who is abandoned. I knew what was expected of me as a daughter and I fulfilled those expectations. I knew what was expected of me as a wife, and I was prepared for that too. I now know what is required of me as a mother, and I'm engaging in that wholeheartedly. But within me lives a woman who is neither a daughter, nor a wife, or a mother. She is independent of all available identities. I don't know what is required of her! I feel lost, like someone who has no structure to lean against. What am I to do with that woman? Where does she belong?"

Guru-Ma smiled brightly and replied with great eagerness, "How about that woman belonging to her own self, my dear? How about you belonging to your self? What if you start taking the responsibility for your own happiness and well being? Yes, my dear Sita, the structure has collapsed for you; and all known pathways have been destroyed; just as they disappeared for me years ago. I simply had to learn to belong to myself and create a pathway that was mine alone. During this long and lonely journey, I felt the deep pain of isolation and there were many times I despaired. But I also felt a sense of liberation to be that person I really was, without fear. I had no fear because I was already alone and there was nothing else that could be taken away from me by anyone anymore. Explore this pathway, my child; see where it will take you. You have nothing to lose; you have already been left alone and you know that you can survive despite your losses. Now follow your heart and re-discover that woman who had been buried under layers and layers of expectations. Liberate her and encourage her to build a structure based on her own internal markings. Such a structure my dear, can never be taken from you, nor can it be destroyed. Have faith, dear Sita, and proceed fearlessly. Life will light up the way that lies ahead of you."

Sita felt a wave of relief at Guru-Ma's words. The possibilities seemed endless, the walkways limitless. She felt an abundant urge to explore and a need to live well. It was not enough just to survive. She could not believe how fortunate she was to have the guidance and love of this enlightened human.

Sita cast a quick glance at Guru-Ma and smiled mischievously! "One last question. Guru-Ma," she said, putting down her sieve and sitting upright. "Was it difficult for you to love Valmiki once he returned to you?"

Noting Guru-Ma's expression, Sita added quickly, "You need not answer this if you feel uncomfortable, kind mother!"

Guru-Ma closed her eyes for a few moments as she smiled slightly. Opening her eyes, she then spoke to Sita in her soft voice, "Sita, I had surrendered all hope that he will ever come back to us ever again. At first I was filled with rage and anguish. Then, as I grew more comfortable in my own resources and in my ability to care for the children, I realized I was not suffering because of his absence any longer. I made peace with my life. My heart loved and was open once again. That is what hearts do my dear, they open and they close, they shut down and refuse to love when they are deeply hurt, and then they open up and learn to love again. It is in the very nature of a heart to do so. I must admit I was attracted to other men every now and then, but because of my independence, I was intimidating to those men; and no long-term relationship ever came out of such mutual attraction. While it was not a pressing need in me, every now and then, I recall, I longed for intimacy with a companion who would treat me with regard and kindness. Even my estranged husband, who I had once loved deeply, did not fit that description anymore."

"When Valmiki returned, he was not the same egoistic human who had left my home. He had tears in his eyes and called me his teacher. Surely trust was eroded and my mind cautioned me against taking him in again. But my heart! Dear Sita, we know so little of our hearts! My heart was humming even as I saw him at the door. Until that moment, I thought I was complete, but then I suddenly felt the soft mist of love, affection, and attraction towards him. I was a bit shocked at myself, dear Sita! How could all this be happening so...quickly? I wondered? Yet by denying my feelings, I would be untrue to myself! Where we are folded we remain unknown to our self! So I decided to take it slowly. I did not rush to embrace him. But I allowed time to either cure or confirm the doubts within me. Sometimes, my dear, when you start living wholeheartedly. The life that is given to you – even though you do not desire for it to be different – brings along everything else that you wish for as well. So yes, it was not as easy but I learned to love him again; and I love him even more deeply now."

The late afternoon sun was descending in the sky. Soon the twins would wake up from their nap. Guru-Ma decided to leave before the boys woke up and again begged her to play with them.

"By the way, I need to get going, dear Sita! Valmiki will be back home and we need to prepare for the evening prayers. I will be back soon enough, my dear. I'm in love with your young sons. And they seem to be in love with me as well." Saying so, Guru-Ma laughed aloud. She hugged Sita once more before taking her leave.

Sita was filled with warmth. A soft sense of happiness prevailed within her body, the kind that is felt when one bears witness to a beautiful thing in nature – a warmth that validates the goodness within you. Enabling you to stay the course in peace and full faith even when facing the unknown. Inside her hut, the boys stirred. Lava whimpered softly. Sita hurried to take care of them.

That night, when the moon emerged into the sky once more, Sita sat in the quiet of her home, searching her thoughts. She reflected on ways in which she could give back to the community that had been so very generous towards her. She wondered about her own unique strengths, and which of those could help strengthen others. She was searching for ways in which she could make a difference in the world. She had a significant education; and that could come in handy if she were to teach these benevolent women and their children. Exhaling softly, she resolved to review her plans with sage Valmiki soon. With that thought, she fell asleep peacefully. Her mind did not race towards any anger that night.

×

XII.

MEDITATION

The huge banyan tree, with its large and leathery leaves, created a canopy of protection from the hot, burning sun. Aerial roots extending from its branches made the banyan tree appear to be upside down. These roots sank downwards, growing deeply into the soil, establishing lateral trunks that grew year after year until some of the subsidiary trunks were much larger and stronger than that of the parent. Standing beneath this natural awning, it was hard to ascertain where this tree started and where it ended. The tree appeared to be a metaphor for life itself!

Right under this large banyan, generations of humans had gathered time and again seeking answers to life's complex riddles. Now, under the cover of its shade, Valmiki held his open classroom. Pupils, young and old, assembled here to acquire knowledge and participate in the discourses. This particular morning the lesson Valmiki would share concerned the art of meditation.

The pre-monsoon sun was still rising in the sky. Lessons had started early that morning, but would end at noon when the blazing sky baked the unshielded earth. The teacher and his students emulated the essence of the banyan; they sat cross-legged upon the uneven earth in one large circle. The students imitated the posture of their teacher, sitting with their backs upright, hands resting on top of their knees with palms turned upward, with eyes closed. This posture, explained Valmiki, was meant to inculcate a sense of openness to life and its vagaries while remaining rooted in the body that acted as a vessel for the soul.

Valmiki instructed them to close their eyes so as to redirect their attention inwards. He advised them to pay attention to the subtle shifts in their consciousness as a result of changes in their thoughts, emotions, and bodily sensations. He then asked them to turn their attention towards their breath alone. With this, the practice of meditation had begun.

Valmiki and his students initiated this ritual with the guttural utterance of the "ohm", which echoed and vibrated in the air as if sanctifying it. The participants sat in silence, focusing upon their breath, observing each inhalation and exhalation for the duration recommended by their master. Valmiki spoke softly, directing them to bring their attention back to their breath with great kindness and without judgment as and when their minds wandered.

The practice continued for a whole hour, with the students redirecting their attention towards their breath as and when their mind strayed.

At the end of an hour, Valmiki initiated the process of training the mind to pay attention to the feeling tones present within the human body. The mind, he explained, was the seat of thoughts and thinking, but it was the body that typically housed all of the emotions and feeling tones. In his soft voice he explained to his disciples that emotions that were avoided, the ones not felt, seemed to be buried alive within the body somehow. He encouraged his students to be aware of their feelings and to grant those feelings the respect they demanded, for otherwise they would outrun the intellect in some inconvenient hour.

Valmiki began in a slow and deliberate manner, "Starting with your feet, notice your toes, each and every one of them ... observe how they feel or simply be aware of a lack of sensation in there ... now guide your attention gently towards the base of your feet and notice what that feels like ... now direct your attention to the top of your feet and your ankles ... slowly move on towards the lower part of your legs, the bone, the calves and the area of your knees ... observe any discomfort in this region ... now gradually move on to your upper legs and your thigh muscles ... pay attention to any tightness or discomfort in here ... gently move your attention to the base of your body and your pelvic region ... observe how the body rests upon the base muscles ... notice for any feelings or sensations in your pelvic region ... now move on to the area of your abdomen, observe the feelings and sensations in your abdomen ... notice how the abdomen rises and falls with your breath ... slowly move your attention towards the back of the abdomen and into the lower back region ... notice any aches or pains in this area, this is the region where the body stores a lot of its stresses and tensions ... pay close attention ... now slowly move onto the area of your upper back and observe how it holds your body ... scan this area for any sensations ... gradually bring your attention towards the front of your chest cavity and the region of your heart ... observe how this area expands and contracts with your breath ... pay attention to feelings of fullness, openness, or any constrictions in this region ... notice any aches or pains within your heart muscles ... now bring your attention to your throat and gradually move on to the back of your neck ... observe how this area holds your head and your body together ... slowly move on to the back of your head and then to the top of your head and observe what this feels like ... now bring your attention to your face and the muscles within ... pay attention to your eyes and your eyeballs ... notice the coolness of the air as the nose inhales and the warmth of the air that is exhaled ... observe your lips and the inner part of your mouth ... pay attention to how the tongue sits in your mouth ... notice the regions of the ears ... feel the expression on your face."

"Now observe your whole body as one unit. Slowly lift your hands and rub your palms together to generate warmth ... place your warm palms upon your eyes and gently massage it ... now gently stroke your whole face and feel the sensation ... placing both the palms together slowly move it to the region of your heart ... gently open your eyes and take in your surroundings ... please repeat after me."

"May I be filled with peace, may my life be free of suffering, may I be filled with happiness and its causes, may I be the cause of happiness and well-being for all ... Namaste ... the life within me pays respect to the life within you." With this Valmiki ended the day's meditation.

The group took a short break before they assembled once again, at which time Valmiki welcomed questions.

"Now the hour is open to any doubts or questions regarding your practice," he announced.

Vedanta, a young disciple who was still new to the practice, posed the first question. "Kind sage Valmiki, even though I start off focusing on my breath, my attention diverts and dances. I find it difficult to rid my mind of its thoughts and am thinking incessantly. Is this a matter that can be resolved with practice? Will I be able to keep my mind free from thinking and focused entirely on my breath during meditation?"

His voice bore a tone of eagerness, though his face revealed slight disappointment in what he presumed to be an imperfection he had observed in his practice.

Valmiki replied, "Freeing the mind of thinking. That would be miraculous. If you, dear Vedanta, can be rid of thoughts during the entire practice and focus only upon your breath, then I will become your student!" A look of surprise lit the face of the young disciple. Valmiki continued, "Dear Vedanta, the human mind is very powerful tool, it will drag you along with thoughts and thinking like a force-filled river because that is what minds do. But this mind has also enabled us to survive, to learn, to impart learning; it is, as you see, an essential tool as well. When you notice your mind drifting during practice, please do not be critical of yourself. Gently, and with love – like a parent caring for an infant – bring your attention back to the breath and continue with the practice. This can happen several times over the period of your practice, but try and bring your attention back each time it occurs. In my own practice, dear Vedanta, I have noticed that over time there have been fewer and fewer thoughts; but even after all these years, I have not been able to rid my mind of thinking during meditation. Know that the quiet your mind experiences in-between two different thoughts is the essence of the practice, and extending this time gap is what you should aim for. Remember it is called the "practice" of meditation. If the mind could be cleared of its habitual thoughts and thinking, there would simply be no need to practice. We are all practicing and will remain practicing for the remainder of our lives "

Hearing these words eased the sense of disappointment that had prevailed in the young student. Listening in fascination, he smiled as he placed his hand upon his chin.

Sumana, a hard-working young mother, diligent in her practice, posed the next question. "Dear Valmiki, you direct us during practice to observe our thoughts and let them go; you instruct us to observe our feelings and let go of them as well. You repeatedly remind us that we are not the same as our thoughts and that we are not the same as our feelings either. And yet you now admit that you too have these thoughts and emotions! Guru, if I am not the same as my thoughts or my emotions then, who am I?"

This question, it was clear to Valmiki, drew the attention of many of his other pupils.

Valmiki smiled as he replied, "Dear Sumana, you are always the curious one! Now let me ask you a question. You confess as well as I that you too observe your thoughts and your feelings during the practice. I assume you observe them even beyond your practice as well. Have you ever wondered who that person is, who is observing all of this from within you? Who is it within you who is observing these thoughts and letting them go? Who is that person who acknowledges all of your feelings and encourages you to let them go? Who is that observer who is unaffected by changes in your internal or external landscape? Now, that person inside of you can surely tell you who it is that you are, my dear child! He is the same observer who is within me, and the one that is within everyone else. Try and pay attention to that one during your practice, sweet Sumana."

On hearing this reply, a look of deep satisfaction came over Sumana's face. She brought her palms to her chest and prostrated herself before her teacher.

Kapila, an aged disciple whose young son had recently died as a result of snakebite, was seated right beside Valmiki. Aggrieved by the unfortunate event that had taken his only child, he had stayed away from his regular practice for a while. Now that he had returned to meditation, he found himself as if starting anew.

"Valmiki, ever since the venomous snake took the life of my young son, my appetite for life has been dwindling!" he confessed in a voice filled with sorrow. "My mind is deeply troubled, and when I sit down to practice it grabs my attention and drags it back to my dead son. I find it impossible to free myself from its power and bring my attention back to my breath. Can you please guide me, for I feel lost!" he pleaded, his eyes filling with tears.

Valmiki's eyes moistened on hearing this. "Kapila, we both go a long way back, and I too miss young Hari who we have lost recently. My loss is not comparable to yours, and I will not try to diminish it by claiming to understand it fully, my dear friend. I am so very happy to see that you have come back to us once more. It shows that you are ready, even though you are still struggling with your sorrow. Kapila, can you please stand up and take a short walk along the banks of the river with the rest of us? We will walk in silence, and we shall walk slowly. Once we come back, you will report to me all that you witnessed within and around you. I will instruct you on your practice once we are back – I promise."

Kapila and the other students followed Valmiki along the banks of the river Tamasa. Valmiki walked with great deliberation, placing each foot carefully on the flat, slanting stones that formed a line to the riverbank. The waters of the river glittered and shone in the sunlight. A slew of thick green vegetation sprang from the rich umber soil; a variety of birds filled the air with the sounds of their calls.

The heavenly blue skies with white foamy clouds casting their grey shadows upon the flowing river invited the song of the fisherman who plied those waters in his rowboat. Where his oars touched the water, it turned to froth, sending out waves of glistening rings that grew bold and then disappeared.

Lured by the scents of sweet flowers and the temptation of fresh fruits, bees flew around as if they were simply floating in air. In the midst of this setting drifted high-pitched voices, the sound of delighted young toddlers. The group noticed that Sita along with her twins – now just a little over one year old – were walking towards the big banyan. The twins stopped at regular intervals to collect souvenirs of leaves and stones, lingering uncounted minutes as they delighted over their find.

Valmiki and his class turned around and headed back to the open-air classroom under the tree. Hampered by the pace of her curious toddlers, Sita knew it would take a while before she could join in the class.

Once they were back, the disciples again formed a circle around their teacher. They waited for the sage to sit before them; then they too took their seats in silence.

Valmiki then turned to Kapila. "Can you describe to me all of your findings in detail?" he asked.

Kapila reported, " Valmiki, the pathway to the river was wet from the drizzle early this morning. I heard birds chirping in the guava trees; saw a bee flitting past me towards the fruit orchards. The river flowed gently and sounded like the giggle of a young child; the oar of the fisherman pushed through the water with a slight roar, and his song was floating in the air long after he was gone. As we returned, I noticed Sita, who was on her way here, and I saw her twin sons picking up leaves and stones along the path. They waved as they smiled at me and spoke in gibberish something which seemed to be very important." Kapila smiled softly at this last observation.

Valmiki questioned him once again, "Kapila, how often did your mind drift towards your grief while you walked with us?"

Kapila thought for a moment before replying, "I must admit that the memory of my son did not pain me as much while I was walking in nature as it did when I sat down in practice with my eyes closed earlier this morning. And when I saw Lava and Kusha my mind ran towards my lost son, but the memory was pleasant. I felt happy for a moment. Then the grief at my son's loss visited me again as we walked back to the big banyan. Lost in thought, I almost stumbled on the smooth stones along the riverbank, at which point I remembered the assignment and came back to noticing the various sights and sounds once more."

Valmiki spoke again. "Kapila, this is to be your practice of meditation from now on. You will walk slowly in nature as you pay close attention to your surroundings. Meditation is the art of paying attention. You can meditate throughout the day by simply being attentive to each happening, moment by moment. Perhaps sitting down with your eyes closed and your focus turned inwards may not be the right practice for you just yet. Once your grief is contained, you can join us back in our sitting practice."

Kapila smiled as he brought the palms of his hands together, displaying his reverence for the master. Once more, tears filled his eyes.

It was almost noon, and the fiery sun was blazing in the sky. Valmiki dismissed the class for the day. With mounting excitement, he prepared to meet the twins, who were now headed in his direction. With their mere presence they seemed to bring him great joy. The disciples stood up and began to leave, one by one, though some lingered around chitchatting with each other. Young Sumana embraced Sita quickly, then picked up the twins and kissed each of them on both cheeks before rushing back home to care for her own children. Valmiki extended his arms as the toddlers rushed towards him and embraced them warmly as he welcomed Sita to his open classroom.

"How are you, my dear Sita? What made you come by here?" he inquired, all the while trying to keep Lava's mischievous hands off his flowing white beard while Kusha tugged at his clothes.

Vani, a young disciple of Valmiki, noticed how her teacher was being teased by the young toddlers and rushed to his aid. With the promise of play, she lured them into the fruit orchard. With a smile, Sita thanked the young woman, acknowledging her thoughtfulness, and promised to come get the boys as soon as she was done speaking with Valmiki.

"Revered Valmiki," Sita said, "I have come to ask for your permission. I am so very grateful for all the help I have received from you, Guru-Ma, and the people of the hermitage. I desire to give back something of value to this community that has been so very generous to me. When I first came here, I was so very lost in my own sorrow that I did not feel I had anything of value to offer. Now I feel differently. I realize I have had the opportunity to get an education that is quite uncommon. My father, King Janaka, was eager to see that his only child was well educated. He had me instructed by the best of teachers and encouraged me to participate in conversations with sages and scholars. I have been instructed in grammar, mathematics, earth sciences, ancient history, Vedic knowledge, poetry, and literature. I was wondering if it would be all right with you if I were to conduct classes to educate some of these women who are willing and eager. Lava and Kusha nap for a full two hours each afternoon, and the women have offered to take turns watching them while I conduct my classes. Enabling these women will help unburden me from the indebtedness I feel towards this community from which I have received so very much."

Her offer seemed to hang in the air as Sita stopped speaking and waited anxiously for a reply.

Valmiki's face lit up. "That is wonderful news, my dear! The hermitage lacks a teacher who is well versed in these many fields of knowledge. Our residents will benefit immensely from having women who are learned and wise like you to instruct them. You can start teaching your students immediately, and as the children grow I would love to see you help me out in my classroom under the big banyan."

Hearing Valmiki's words. Sita was filled with great joy. She had lost her family by blood in her marriage to Rama. She had lost the family she was married to because of wild rumors. But now she felt as if she had gained a family of kindred spirits! She felt safe! These were her people, and this place was her home. She thanked Valmiki for providing her this wonderful opportunity and excused herself. As she walked hastily towards her children, she felt as if they were the reason her heart beat and her blood flowed each day.

Valmiki exhaled softly as he watched Sita join her young ones. His heart was filled with paternal pride, and his eyes grew moist. Truly Sita was one of the most courageous women of his time.

×

XIII.

EMPOWERMENT

Sita felt as if her life had taken a new curve, bending in a different direction. It was like following a narrow, long walkway surrounded by thick vegetation, threading amidst the tall woods, then suddenly turning into a vast open landing where she could behold a view of valleys and sun-drenched mountains in the distance. A life that had felt arrested fixed in the here and now, had broadened into an expanse of endless abundance.

Sita was meticulous in her preparation for her classes. She resolved, early on, what would be her style of instruction. She would provide guidance not by pointing directions or clinching arguments but with a fullness, a many sided openness, that would surely enable her students to make up their own minds. This approach, she concluded, would harness the inner richness of each individual, strengthening their ability to see with their own eyes, choose with their own minds, and formulate a purpose that was unique.

All women willing to learn were grouped in different classes based on their previous skills and education. Sita formulated a curriculum that was broad and encompassing, affording ample scope to specialize in preferred fields of learning. She often worked with sages and scholars who visited the hermitage, drawing forth from them new ideas and opinions.

Finally, after nearly six months of preparation, Sita launched her classes at the end of the monsoons.

The afternoon classes filled Sita with a sense of power and gave her a fervor that she had not fully expected. Previously, dreams of her childhood had stood like a haze in the distance, veiling her restless urge to spread out and live. Now she felt the demand to fully embrace those dreams. Every little feature that had been subdued during years of careful grooming now stood out boldly and clearly. Even to her, it was a surprise to find her voice in each one of them, shimmering with aliveness. Sita's beauty was now shattering, like light passing through a prism, and as she gathered all of the different rays with an eager hunger, she realized how rich she felt for the very first time.

The classes began on the front porch of Sita's hut in the hermitage. Sitting upon the bare earth on straw mats, the first five women – making their first attempt to acquire an education – seemed eager and excited. Clad in saris, with flowers in their hair and jingling bangles upon their wrists, they started by learning how to enunciate each letter of the alphabet. Sita patiently initiated the pronunciation of the vowels – a, ā, i, ī, u, ū, which was repeated all afternoon. At the end of the class, Sita handed out their assignments, and they bid her goodbye after making a humble offering of fruit and food, which was customary for students showing appreciation to their "Gurus." The next round of lessons for this group would be held the same day the following week, and at the same time.

The next afternoon, eight young women who knew their alphabet and could read a little came for their classes. The objective of the classes, for this group of women, was fluency and comprehension. Sita worked with these women by first showing them words handwritten on wood parchment. They practiced with short and long sentences all afternoon. As she had done with the previous group, Sita assigned her students specific practices for the week ahead. She would meet this group once again the following week.

The next day, Sita's class was composed of four students who were well versed in reading and writing but lacked knowledge of the general arts and sciences. Sita taught these women about the different constellations, the position of the stars in the sky, and the science of figuring out distance and angles. These four women were her more advanced students. In her own mind Sita had established the intention of soon preparing these to serve as teachers and assistant teachers at the hermitage. In the curriculum for this class, Sita had planned advanced lessons in the mathematics of trade, the geometry of construction, astronomy, ayurvedic sciences, literature, rules of grammar, and the science of political wisdom.

On the fourth afternoon, all of her students – irrespective of the classes to which they belonged – gathered together. They sang songs woven from lines of poetry and chanted verses from Vedic texts that Sita had explained and translated for them. At the end of this class, there was always an open discussion when the assembled women were provided with the opportunity to raise any issues or concerns and seek solutions. This encouraged and enabled them to stay committed to the process of learning and acquiring an education.

Within a year, word of these classes had spread, and the number of students wishing to attend increased exponentially. Sita had to move her venue to the big banyan.

There are trees that grow straight like arrows from the earth towards the sky, standing like pillars in the wind, refusing to be harnessed. Filled with assurance about their solitary existence, they neither crave company nor do they pity their plight; they occupy a heaven of their own where they will be saved or face a personal hell for their own damnation. Then there are those other trees – the ones that interlock their branches and harmonize their roots to form an everlasting embrace. Their strength is in their mutual grasping and their unwillingness to let go. Each victory is multiplied by the victories of others in their community, and they die having passed on every fiber of their strength to the ones that remain standing. Sita felt as if she was such a tree, one that was strengthening the community around her.

The knowledge she imparted to her dedicated students lighted lamps, big and small, all over the hermitage. Within a few years there were visible changes in the lives of citizens at the hermitage. Children of literate mothers came to school knowing their letters and numbers; they sang songs of historic achievements and parroted poetry they had heard at home. Bedtimes were enriched by imaginative stories, narrated by their mothers, which enabled these new saplings to anchor their dreams in places that had been unknown to their ancestors. Their self-esteem was bolstered as they acquired greater skills and gained knowledge of fundamental mathematics, and these women boosted local commerce. Gifts in the form of bushels of vegetables, sacks of rice and wheat, milk and butter, clay utensils and reams of cotton flowed into the hermitage in exchanges that reflected the education imparted impartially to everyone. By nourishing souls that nourished homes, Sita introduced wholesomeness to her own life and the lives of her children. Lava and Kusha, who were now five years old, were ready to start their own education.

The twin boys had grown beautifully and were deeply cared for by the residents of the hermitage. Incredibly handsome, with sparkling brown eyes and thick, wavy black hair that curled down at the shoulders; they were curious, spirited, and friendly. Lava, the older one, was drawn to instinctive action while Kusha leaned towards reflective contemplation. Needless to say, it was quite apparent that these young lads were destined for a future that was larger than anyone could imagine!

The mango grove in the northeastern corner of the hermitage was designated for the practice of archery. Young boys were introduced to this art form as a way to inculcate in them the needed skills of self-defense and discipline. Three large trees had been marked for practice, with circular targets crafted out of hay and ropes – each marked at the center – were nailed to the tree trunks of these three trees. If a young man shot three arrows consecutively at the center of the targets, then he earned all the mangoes that he and his classmates had harvested that day.

Lava, filled with boisterous energy and a crazed desire to master the arts of warfare, often hid in the grove watching the archers as they practiced with deep concentration. The atmosphere was quiet, with each archer showing a keen attentiveness. Filing in, the archers formed a neat line; each had a bow in hand and three arrows in a pouch carried upon their shoulders. As each stepped forward to take aim, the others stood back and observed in silence. Posture, breath, strength, and action had to be synchronized to achieve the desired objective. Taking up his position, a boy would step forward on his left foot, placing the right behind the shooting line, his feet parallel to the line and a shoulder-length apart. With his chin rotated over the shoulder of the arm that held the bow, the boy would straighten his lower back while his upper body was thrust downwards.

Assuming this stance, the archer had his eye set on a target that was aligned precisely with the tip of the arrow. The string was pulled back with calculated strength and force, and then released, sending the arrow onto the target.

Some of the boys succeeded in getting one or two arrows onto the central marking; most managed to shoot in the vicinity of the target, bringing down mangoes in the process. Being able to hit the center of the target many times in succession was an indication of consistent precision and a sign of progression towards the mastery that these young men sought so eagerly.

Having slipped away from his home once again, Lava – who was observing these young men from a distance – was pining for some action of his own. The fact that other children of his age were not practicing archery did not deter him; it simply meant that he would have to be a pioneer! He had studied each of the practicing students attentively several times and had secretly picked up nuances of the skill.

The young men, after a taxing morning of continuous practice, piled up their arrows, placed their bows upon a wooden rack, and departed one by one as their day's lessons were done. With the grove now deserted, Lava was tempted to try his hand.

It was late morning when Sita noticed with dismay that her precocious older twin was missing once again. Seeing Kusha playing with his friends, Sita drew him aside to question him about his twin's whereabouts. Not wishing to reveal what his brother was up to, Kusha feigned complete ignorance of Lava's absence, even though he knew precisely where his twin brother was. Knowing better than to trust him, Sita threatened Kusha with severe consequences if he did not come clean, and she was partially amused to note that he did not waver.

Ridden with anxiety about her missing child, Sita loudly called out his name, turning in every direction. Soon everyone who was anyone was searching for Lava while Kusha waited for the right opportunity to slip away to the mango grove to warn his brother. From a distance Sita saw Valmiki waving. He beckoned her ferociously as if asking her to make haste. Panicked, filled with fear, she ran towards Valmiki, certain that her child was in grave trouble. As she neared him, Valmiki placed his index finger over his lip indicating for her to be quiet. Then he pointed in the direction of the mango groove.

Taking her place alongside Valmiki who was hidden behind a large tree trunk, Sita watched in silence, observing Lava at his mischief.

He had picked up a bow from the rack and had slung a quiver with a handful of arrows across his shoulder. With a brilliant posture and seemingly unfailing concentration, he leveled the bow and drew back the string, letting arrows fly one at a time. A good majority of the arrows struck the target very close to the center! Yet this was a child who had never had a day's lesson in archery! Sita's eyes shone, reflecting equal measures of pride and fear, while Valmiki smiled gleefully at the little one's accomplishment. Little brother Kusha, who had followed his mother, put both his hands upon his open mouth as if to hold back an excited squeal. He worried about the trouble the two of them might get into, Lava for picking up the bow and arrow and him for concealing Lava's whereabouts!

Sita looked more and more anxious as she watched the young boy. "I am afraid that he might hurt someone!" she whispered softly. "Besides, I do not wish for either of them to be warriors or to fight in battles," she muttered.

But she was convincing no one! Valmiki turned around to look at her, now with a smile on his face.

"What I wish is for them to be men of learning and wisdom! I do not know how I can dissuade Lava from his willfulness. I have tried so very often to introduce him to other interests and pursuits. But he seems adamant to pick fights for the slightest reason." Sita spoke in haste, her voice filled with deep concern.

Valmiki shook his head as he whispered back to her, "Look at your child Sita! Look into his curious heart that badly wants to learn and explore! What do you think he needs?"

Sita returned Valmiki's look, a bit puzzled and overly concerned. Her anxious mind raced to find answers. Was Valmiki suggesting that young Lava needed his father? Was he indicating that she was not a good mother – or was it simply a proposition to get young Lava enrolled in archery lessons?

Valmiki, noticing her bewilderment, smiled as he replied, "All I'm saying is that the boys are becoming self-aware. And you, as their mother, are solely responsible for smoothing their rough edges. It is not becoming of you to try and set them upon a track that is different from the one they are born into."

Looking into her curious face, he continued, "Sita, nature is irrepressible! If it is not honored, it creates unnecessary suffering amongst people. If a fish is asked to climb a tree, the fish will not only fail but will assume that it is incompetent and incapable of anything good. These children, your children, have a temperament and interests that are their own. They will grow into their unique selves spontaneously, provided they are not hindered. Love them for who they are, for their strengths and weaknesses alike. This will enable each one to know that his true self is lovable and acceptable, it will make them secure. By doing so, you will be enabling them to make choices that are appropriate and to engage in pursuits that provide them with a meaningful existence. Self-awareness allows each person to know and trust his role in the intricate matrix of life. Ponder on these words, my dear, before we officiate their learning at school. Live within your doubts and questions until you find the answers within you. You cannot teach the children something that you don't believe is true."

So saying, Valmiki left Sita, who stood gazing at her young.

Even fine achievements need to be marked with a hint of censure, especially when are accomplished by someone who is not thinking through the likely consequences. When Sita called out his name, Lava turned in surprise. Instantaneously, smiling nervously, he lied, "I was just holding the bow and arrow, Mother! I wanted to know what it felt like!"

Kusha broke in quickly: "We already watched you shoot the arrows, Lava. Mother was shocked but she seemed happy. I tried to warn you, but sage Valmiki had already seen you in the mango grove, and he let mother know."

"Oh! So you knew Lava was here?" asked Sita, now staring down at Kusha.

Both boys bent their heads and apologized softly. They followed their mother back home. After that, they had to stay indoors; missing out on playtime and snacks for the rest of the day. Eager to earn back the favor of their mother – who seemed upset for no great reason – they did her bidding faithfully. When Sita invited them to eat their dinner, they were pleased to find her smiling. They hugged and kissed her, promising they would never lie to her again. Little did they know that she was never really upset to begin with.

After a long, tiring day filled with all kinds of excitement, Sita sat before her sleeping boys and watched them intently. They were growing up quickly! They were beginning to ask questions. She recalled how, a few weeks back on a windy afternoon all the children of the hermitage had been out flying kites in the fields nearby. A child of the neighbors had gone to his father asking him for help with his kite. "My father can do anything!" he had boasted, to which Kusha had quickly replied, "So can my mother!" After a long afternoon of kite-flying competition, Kusha had asked her about "fathers." His exact words had been, "Why do some of my friends have a father and a mother?", "Why do those families need two adults?" Sita had burst out laughing at his innocent questions. Kusha had rejoiced in the feeling of having caused his mother to laugh even though he did not fully understand why.

Sita stroked the faces of her sleeping sons as she pondered the words spoken by sage Valmiki earlier in the day. She looked intently, with great love, at the small hands of the sleeping Lava. These small hands had accomplished an incredible feat at archery that very morning! Certainly he was born to be a fine warrior like his father. Dissuading him would be meddling and would not help him in any way. Perhaps it was time for the boys to know about their father. They were destined to be rulers like him; she could see that from their inclinations and pursuits. Even Sita would not be able to keep them from their destiny. As a mother, she could enable them to follow their chosen pursuits and not stand in their way. But she knew this already. This was not what had been bothering her all day long.

"What is it that you are really afraid of?" she asked herself in the darkness of the moonless night.

She tossed and turned in her bed, unwilling to admit that she already knew the answer. She was afraid that she would lose the boys someday. She was afraid their destiny would take them away from her. She was terrified at the prospect of having to be alone once again. She was reluctant to admit the pain that was inevitably to be hers. All of her accomplishments, her successes, her learning, her wisdom, her children, her students, and her charity – none of this protected her from her feelings of aloneness. Her fear-filled mind grasped for comfort. She would plead with her children and never allow them to leave her. She would speak with Lava and encourage him to give up his desire for warfare. She would persuade the boys to accept a life that would always keep them close to her. She would surely wither away and die if they left her. Sita exhaled loudly, then laughed.

It was sheer foolishness. None of this would work. Life would press on, barging in like a river in full spate, dragging along everything in its current! She could choose to swim along with the flow, having faith that she and her precious children would be all right, or she could suffer and cause suffering to her young sons by trying to fight the current! Sita knew what had to be done.

X

XIV.

INITIATION

Sita woke up happy; her work and her love for her children made life promising and filled her with hope. She was no longer a lonely princess reigning over dreams she had conjured. Now she felt she was one among an army of women, a simple human in service to ideas that were beneficial to all. Everywhere she went, she was welcome, respected, and loved.

With Lava and Kusha now five years old, it seemed as if time had simply sailed by. Sita held precious memories of all the happiness and safety that had been woven into the picturesque landscape of family life! She fondly recalled the manner in which Lava and Kusha had held hands as they had taken their first steps together, the first time they had called her "Mother," the eagerness in her chest as she waited to hear their voices speaking complete sentences, the joy she felt when she heard them pronounce the alphabets merely from having heard it in her classes, the tenderness with which they stroked the newborn calf, her own amusement when – barely being able to walk steadily on their own feet – they had attempted to carry her in their arms.

Now they were old enough to start formal lessons, and Sita's heart beat wildly with excitement. The possibilities seemed endless; her wishes and dreams for her sons as fathomless as the ocean! Sita woke up early and sat gazing at the jasmine creeper edging its way into her home through the window. She smiled warmly as she stroked the faces of her beautiful children and kissed them, nudging them to wake up. The big day had come.

Looking radiant in her red sari, her face framed by braided hair hanging down her left shoulder, Sita looked as glorious as the early morning sun. She walked gracefully to the big banyan, accompanying Lava and Kusha. The boys were clad in white garments; their hair had been brushed neatly behind their ears, and each wore the mark of red vermillion on their foreheads.

Sita brought in a plate filled with fruits and flowers as offering to Valmiki and Guru-Ma who, as elders in the community, were to initiate the learning ceremony. Guru-Ma received her warmly, and let Sita and the twins into her home. Sumantha, a young teacher responsible for the education of the youngest children in the hermitage, sat patiently waiting.

Beside him was Valmiki, sitting upon a thin mat, preparing two lamps to be lit. He placed the cotton wicks at the center of painted clay lamps filled with ghee, then instructed Lava and Kusha to sit patiently by their mother. He directed Sita to light one of the lamps while naming it for her older twin son.

Valmiki handed a copper plate filled with grains of rice to Sita as he said, "The mother is always the first teacher of her child. "

After these words he instructed Sita to hold Lava's right hand and write the "ohm" upon the grains of rice; this, he explained, was to invite the blessings of the Gods. After that, each letter of the alphabet was traced one by one. The same ritual was repeated with Kusha who had been waiting eagerly for his turn. With this, formal lessons for the boys had begun.

Sumantha then held the hands of Lava and Kusha and directed them towards their class under the big banyan. The boys hugged Sita, then enthusiastically followed in the footsteps of their teacher. Several of their friends and neighbors were also in this class, and they giggled excitedly at the prospect of soon joining them.

As she watched them walk away from her, Sita's eyes grew moist and nervous excitement filled her heart.

Valmiki, noticing her tears, asked in a gentle tone, "What do you think the boys need from you?"

Brushing aside her tears, Sita replied, "I realize what is needed from me, kind sage, it is my heart that is at times unwilling to part with them. Each of my children needs an understanding of his unique self; they need to honor the gifts that they are born with. This is the primary lesson that a mother can impart to a child. Loving them for who they are will enable them to have faith in their own abilities and resources. I have resolved to do what is right by them, but I will need your help in making sure that I myself do not stand in their way, kind Valmiki."

As Sita continued, her voice was filled with worry, "Kind sage, what if self-awareness results in self-indulgence and they become uncaring and overly absorbed in themselves? How do I prevent this?"

Sighing, Valmiki looked away from Sita into the distance, as if searching for the right words. "Yes, my dear Sita, parenting is rife with anxious thinking, I can understand your worry. The purpose of self-awareness is not self-aggrandizement or indulgence, Sita, it is simply to equip them with tools to navigate through their life. Its purpose is to make known and bring into awareness one's unique strengths and one's weaknesses. Just as you provide them with good nourishment, proper discipline, an extensive education and love, self-awareness is also a tool enabling them to live with acceptance of who they are."

Valmiki continued, "If Lava is a warrior, encourage his inner inclinations but also educate him in the discipline of diplomacy and pragmatism, empower him with mindful meditation, encourage him to pay attention to the wisdom of his counsel, but most of all teach him to not lose faith in his instincts. If Kusha is contemplative and quiet, emphasize the powers of his introversion, educate him in the importance of expression and action and empower him by giving him practice in the arts of debate and discourse. Sita, the boys are growing up in a hermitage modeled on compassion and love, they wake up each day in a home with a prudent, wise and caring mother. Have faith my dear! They will face challenges like everyone else, but they will be better equipped than most to deal with these challenges."

Observing Guru-Ma watching him, Valmiki quickly added, "Of course this is something that I learned from my wife, and it is what I have started to do with my grandchildren. A man has to start somewhere – does he not, my dear? As you may well know, my own children were already grown by the time I got back to my family."

He chuckled nervously as he looked at his attentive wife. Guru-Ma, smiled and shook her head!

"Be kind to you, Valmiki!" said Guru-Ma with a soft smile upon her face.

"About that!" exclaimed Sita. "The boys have been asking me questions about their father. I might have to tell them about him soon!"

Her voice was anxious. Guru-Ma looked at Valmiki, her expression filled with concern.

She then turned towards Sita and asked in a soft voice, "Are you still angry at King Rama, dear Sita?"

Sita thought in silence for a moment before she answered, "Not anymore Guru-Ma! My anger faded into a vague disappointment, which has disappeared into acceptance. I now accept my life as it has come to me and feel great gratitude for everything in it. It almost seems to me that my suffering was necessary to bring forth the woman who was hidden within. Today I am not just an obedient queen, relegated to the backdrop of her husband's life. Today I am a woman who is making life better for others like myself. The love that I receive from my students enriches me and makes me feel fulfilled. So, no, I do not feel anger anymore. In fact, when I think of Rama I wish him much happiness and well-being."

"Then what is it that you desire to tell the children, dear Sita?" asked Guru-Ma. Sita did not hesitate.

"The truth!" she replied.

Guru-Ma smiled at Sita knowingly. "Now tell me, dear Sita, what is it that you fear?"

Sita exhaled and closed her eyes for a few minutes. When she again turned to face Guru-Ma, her eyes were filled with tears. "I fear that I will lose my children, Guru-Ma. I fear my aloneness in their absence. I fear that I might not have done everything rightly by them and that they will suffer as a result of it."

Sita's voice was quivering with fear and resignation.

Guru-Ma responded, "Letting go and feeling alone! ... Perhaps these hard things are made harder and more difficult for us women. ... After all, nature has entrusted us with the task of bringing new life into the world, caring for it, and making it strong and viable. ... Nature is irrepressible! The nature within the life that we help create – that is irrepressible, too! That life we nurture has to step out and express its self fully. You can step aside and share in the happiness of its glorious blooming or you can hold onto it and suffocate its growth. ... I don't for a moment doubt that you do not know the right thing to do in this instance, Sita! And even I cannot protect you from feeling alone."

Guru-Ma hesitated then continued, "What has helped me, my dear Sita, is to enlarge my heart and extend its favors. When the only family you know is the family under your roof, you live in fear that you'll lose them. When your sense of family extends to the world outside, there are always enough things to be done and there is always someone to care for. You too, will find your way my dear. Have faith!"

Valmiki chuckled, softly, "The boys are not going anywhere anytime soon! They have just started to go to school! And the two of you women are brooding over what is going to happen years from now when neither of you barely know that which will happen the next moment... Well, I am done with my work here and have to attend to my teachers in their lessons. Come along Sita; hurry up my dear! Your students must be waiting!"

So saying, he left in haste.

Sita smiled and took her leave. As she turned to go, Guru-Ma said, "The truth was what I told my children my dear!"

That night, during dinner, Lava and Kusha shared vivid descriptions of their experiences in school, taking great delight in their tales. At the end of the day when Sita readied them for bed, they pleaded with her to tell them a story. In her own mind, Sita had already prepared one, and now she sat down to narrate that story to her children.

"A long time ago a beautiful baby was born to the great king of Mithila, King Janaka. She was loved dearly by her father and lived in a huge palace with an abundance of comforts. The king made sure the princess had everything. She took baths in warm waters perfumed with flowers; she wore the best of silks, fancy jewelry and had several playmates and pets. She was given a fine education in all matters of administering an empire and appreciating the arts. She enjoyed a life that was carefree and pleasant in its simplicity. Soon she grew up to be a beautiful young lady.

"One day her father told her it was time for her to embrace her destiny and serve as queen of a large empire. He told her that he would arrange for a magnificent contest, and only a prince who was extremely skilled and intelligent would be allowed to marry her. The princess's young heart was torn between anxiety at leaving her home and feeling curious about this magnificent prince who would bring joy into her life. She dreamed about him that very night: she dreamt that he would love her deeply and that their love would be so deep and satisfying that she would never need anything ever again during her whole life. She dreamt that he would be strong, brave, skillful, intelligent, and yet sensitive in his heart and supremely kind. And sure enough he was. The prince, who won the contest, was able to lift a very heavy bow and string it easily!"

Lava interrupted, "So, Mother, did he really do that? He must have been a great archer then. Do you think I will be as good someday? Sorry for interrupting – please continue with the story."

Sita smiled as she continued, "Soon there was a great celebration and the beautiful princess married the handsome prince. They were happy for a while, but the prince got banished to the forest for fourteen years by his father, as his stepmother wanted the kingdom for her son. The princess left – along with the prince – to go into the forest, leaving behind all their belongings. In the forest they lived in a tiny hut."

"Just like us – right. Mother?" Kusha asked.

Sita nodded before continuing. "But they were happy just like we are now. In the forest the young prince had more time to spend with the princess, and the clever princess was creative and provided a lot of fun for them. They ate simple food that she cooked lovingly and got to know each other very well. They listened with great care to the stories of their childhood days. Their hopes, dreams, and love for each other deepened. One day when the prince went deep into the forest to hunt, the princess – after finishing all her chores – sat in the front porch of their small hut waiting for him. An evil demon dressed as a sage came to the hut and begged for some food. When the kind-hearted princess went towards him to offer some of their food, the demon captured her, threw her into his chariot, and sped away"

"What!!!", both children cried at the same moment.

"Oh! Mother that is so sad!", exclaimed Kusha.

"Go, on don't stop please tell us the rest of it!", urged Lava, who had now moved closer to Sita.

Sita stopped. Closing her eyes, she allowed her breath to flow more evenly and observed her emotions. The pain had grown a scab; she had survived her ordeal and was now thriving. But like all events that change life in its entirety in a single moment, the seed of pain still lay within her heart, even though she had long given up nurturing it. She put her hand upon her heart and consoled the young, helpless woman who had suffered so very deeply. She sent kindness to that young prince who had lost his beautiful wife.

Sita continued, "The prince loved the princess deeply and decided to fight with the demon. He assembled a whole army and marched to the island where the demon resided in his huge palace. The princess was held captive in one of the gardens there, her heart was broken, and she cried every single day. The prince secretly sent out a spy who informed the princess that she would soon be rescued. He sent his finger ring along with the spy, so the princess would know the message was for real. She smiled for the first time in several days. Soon, a mighty war commenced. Both sides fought valiantly, and many people died. But the prince, being a very skilled warrior, defeated the demon and crushed him to the ground. Now released, the princess ran into the arms of her husband. They cried tears of joy as they embraced each other. They were delighted to be reunited."

"That is beautiful!" exclaimed Lava.

"Please continue. Don't stop!" urged Kusha.

Sita smiled sadly at her children. "The fourteen years of living in the forest had come to an end, and the prince and the princess went back to their empire. The stepmother's plans had failed as her son loved the prince and readily gave back the empire to him. Everything seemed to be working out just fine. But sadness was beginning to creep silently into their hearts. The princess did not laugh with wild abandon anymore – as she was afraid – and the young prince felt alone when he was with her as he could not understand her sadness. The prince felt hurt that he could not make her happy as he had done before and was a bit angry with her and with himself. He spent more and more time at his work, and his fame grew. But every now and then someone would comment on the impurity of the princess because she had been abducted and forced to live with another man. These comments hurt the prince deeply. When the princess heard what was being said, she grew sadder and suffered great pain. She wanted the prince to acknowledge her pain and her hurt feelings. She wanted him to hold her and tell her that he too felt sad when he heard such comments. She wanted him to tell her that he loved her, and to stay with her for as long as it would take for her to feel safe once again. The prince, however, pretended to be brave in front of his wife. He wanted her to forget the past and start afresh; he did not want to be angry with her for something that she had been unable to prevent. He wanted to be happy once again, just as they were when they lived in the forest. But somehow, though they wanted to be happy again, they could not figure out how."

"That's easy, Mother, they just have to sit down and talk and show how much they care about each other, like we do here, right?" asked Kusha. Sita nodded sadly in agreement.

"But they were not taught to do this, Kusha. The princess had been told to please her husband, no matter what, and she did her best to pretend that everything was all right even when she hurt deeply inside. The prince had been taught to be brave in all situations, and he did not know what to do when he felt sad and helpless. But sooner or later, what is in the heart overflows and floods the mind, and in the power of these forceful emotions wisdom is side-stepped."

"Anyway, once when a washer-man criticized the prince for having a wife who had lived with another man, the prince felt even more deeply afflicted. It was apparent to him, now, that all his subjects were apprehensive about his choice of a wife. So he ordered the princess – who was pregnant with her children – to leave the kingdom immediately. And soon she was abandoned in the forest."

"Oh! Stop, Mother, this story is getting sadder by the minute!", protested Lava. "I hate that prince. How could he be so cruel? If Valmiki were there, he would protect the princess and tell the subjects to mind their own business."

Sita smiled, "Dear child, try not to judge the events of the past, but learn from them. You are a brave, strong young boy, and your brother is wise and prudent. The two of you can show the world a new way to experience life. Perhaps the prince and the princess suffered so that Kusha and Lava could grow up with a brand new set of ideals. Guess what! Valmiki rescued the princess! The kind people of the hermitage have taught her much. Her heart is open and loving. She is not afraid anymore. She is graceful, she is kind, and she laughs with abandon once again."

"Oh! Mother!" The two exclaimed.

"So this is your story. And the prince is our father?" Kusha's eyes grew wide as he asked the question.

Sita smiled and nodded once again. Lava jumped up to hold her securely in his arms, and a moment later Kusha joined in their embrace. The three held each other tightly, feeling in their hearts an abundance of love, gratitude, pain, and inner strength. At that moment Sita knew that her children would be all right.

✕

XV.

A FUTURE BEYOND

Twelve years had passed since the birth of the twin boys Lava and Kusha! Sita sat in quiet contemplation, warmed by the fire in her kitchen. It was nighttime and her sons were fast asleep. Sita noticed how her beautiful brown hair was intertwined with strands of silver. Her radiant face had creases around her black eyes. She was leaner, and her limbs were muscular and strong from hard work. Her hands were no longer soft and supple, they felt infused with an inner strength and confidence. Sita felt like a complete woman now, comfortable in her ways, self-aware, beautiful, calm, loving and yet vulnerable.

Twelve years before, her world had decomposed, all structures had disappeared, all rules abandoned, all hopes vanquished. She had assumed she would die. Back then; she had believed that she would never know happiness again. Now Sita sat reflecting upon how very little we know of our self and our lives. She smiled at the innumerable moments she had spent anxiously fearing the ultimate catastrophe of physical death while ignoring her own ability to survive the innumerable deaths of her identity that would occur over the span of a lifetime.

If she had been told, twelve years before, that she would give birth to two healthy babies, that she would make a home for them on her own, that she would impart knowledge to countless women and – most importantly – that she was to know happiness once again, she would have never believed it!

Sita felt gratitude – gratitude towards the community that had embraced her and helped her build her home, gratitude for her children who gave her much love and a great sense of purpose in her life. And she felt a surprising amount of gratitude for the suffering that her life had brought to her, the suffering that enabled her to become the woman she was today. That suffering had freed her soul from the restraints of her mind. She stopped to notice how happiness had simply flowed into her life once she had stopped pursuing it! And now that twelve years had passed, she had to think about the future of her children.

Lava and Kusha had grown handsomely! The boys were as tall as Sita now! Care was received from them as well as being provided by her. Sita smiled at how the boys had stopped her from going down to the well for water; they had assumed this responsibility two years before, and had been diligent. Lava had climbed on top of the roof and fixed the leak last week, stirring Sita's admiration. Kusha always made sure that there was ample firewood for their home.

The twins sported shoulder-length hair that was curled into waves along the edges. Lava's broad face, with its sharp nose and mesmerizing brown glittering eyes, instantaneously brought him the attention he craved! He was outgoing and friendly, eager to please, and adored – particularly by the older women at the hermitage with whom he often joked and laughed. Kusha's face was oval, unlike his brother's, but his features were equally handsome! His incisors overlapped a bit, and that feature – along with the deep dimples that kissed his smooth cheeks – made him immensely attractive when he smiled. A bit shyer than his overbearing brother, he was immensely favored by his teachers and fellow students. Both boys paid great attention to their appearance. Dressed in bright orange and green hand-printed jackets with white dhotis, displaying muscular bodies and neatly combed hair curling at the neck and shoulders, they were the admiration of one and all.

Needless to say, Sita's heart overflowed with love at the mere thought of her young sons.

In the hermitage, Lava had acquired all the available skills in the arts of warfare. His interests had started with archery and extended to fencing, wrestling, horse riding, and – surprisingly – history. He knew every detail of every war ever fought on the land and had studied assiduously to discover the causes for each success and reasons for every defeat. Eager to become the best swordsman and archer in the country, he was tempted to pursue skills taught to young princes and kings outside of the hermitage in faraway cities where there were acclaimed schools and institutions.

Kusha had an insatiable appetite for learning as well. He too had exhausted most of the resources available to him at the hermitage. Though Sita had fortified his education with additional lessons, she was acutely aware that she did not have very much more to offer to her prodigious young son. Young Lava was tempted and excited by the prospect of attending other institutions of learning outside the hermitage. The twin boys were getting ready to fulfill their destinies.

Sita had to make the tough choice of allowing them liberty to fully follow their dreams. Perhaps the time had come for her to approach King Rama. She could not enable the twins' development any further, and she loved them so deeply that she did not wish to stand in the way of their happiness.

Sita decided to approach Valmiki to discuss her plans with him. She would do it the very next day. This was something that could not be put off any longer.

Morning came, like all mornings, gushing forth into life, shattering the safety of darkness and demanding action. Lava and Kusha had slept with their blankets drawn tightly against their bodies, and now Sita covered them with her own blanket as she readied herself for her practice of meditation. Wrapped in a coarse red shawl, she sat in silent meditation enjoying the warmth of the kitchen furnace. She sat cross-legged upon the floor, back erect and eyes closed. Her mind was intensely focused upon her breath, and she was fully present to her practice. She visualized a bright light within herself and focused on its radiance. Soon it radiated all through her body and then beyond her body to the universe outside. For a few moments she experienced a state of dissolution within a field of energy that felt indiscriminate and universal – an energy that lacked judgment, seemed endless in its flow and unknown in its origin. It felt as if the flow of time had stopped, the past like the future stood erased, with this sacred energy reviving her moment by moment. Sita sat without stirring, feeling safety in its knowledge, assimilating the texture of its neutrality.

Like everyone blessed with a mind, Sita found that hers soon diverted her attention to the decision of introducing her children to their father. Just as soon as the thought entered, she felt a tremor in her heart as her body experienced the anxiety of losing her precious children. Sita simply labeled the emotion, without judgment. She was experiencing anxiety. As she studied the texture of her thought, she saw it was focused on the future. Sita gently brought back her attention to her breath once again. She continued with her practice until she heard the temple bells in the distance. It was time to start her day's work.

Sita prepared breakfast for herself and her sons as the boys bathed, dressed, and offered their morning prayers. She had decided to visit Guru-Ma and Valmiki and seek their help regarding her decision to approach Rama.

Guru-Ma sat upon the floor right in the path of a beam of sunlight that found its way into her home spilling through the small window. The morning light was resplendent, and her aged face glowed in its mystery. She had used her wooden comb to part her hair right in the center of her forehead, like as she had always done. Pressing the thin, silver strands against her scalp, she gathered the remaining length of her hair and drew it carefully to the back of her head where she rolled it into a tight bun. Next she fenced in this bun with a string of jasmine flowers. Finally, she dipped her forefinger into the small jar of red vermillion paste and placed it in the center of her forehead, right between her eyebrows. As she examined herself in the mirror, she felt satisfied with her appearance.

Valmiki dipped his head into the clean waters of the flowing river one last time. Standing in its waters with a thin wrap around his waist, palms folded, facing the east, he offered his prayers to the rising sun. With slow, deliberate footsteps, he entered the bank, where he dressed himself before he made his way towards his home. He noted with kind compassion how much fatigue he felt in his aging body as he simply went about his daily routine.

Valmiki recognized Sita walking in the direction of his home, and he welcomed her warmly. Her fingers were interlaced in nervous anticipation as she rubbed her palms together. He smiled broadly, as if – having read her mind instantaneously – he wanted to reassure her.

"No man dips in the same river twice, my dear." he said. "Our identity is evolving incessantly, and the river, too, is flowing with different waters every second. With each dip that a man takes in the river, both he and the river are different! What comes together will always disperse, and things that are dispersed come back together in new ways."

Valmiki paused and attended to his breath. He had found the walk to the river and back getting more strenuous with each passing day. Sita slowed her pace to accommodate him and extended her hand for him to hold. He smiled with gratitude as he took her hand and resumed walking.

"My dear Sita, please do not assume that this old man who seems to provide you with wisdom does not suffer from longings just like you do. I will be devastated if my frail wife is taken from me. Try holding onto others gently. Hold on gently to that which you love so you create space for the course that life has bestowed upon it. Hold on gently to that which you cherish so as to enjoy the beauty that is unique to its nature. Hold on gently to that which you assume is yours so that the collective consciousness can exhale comfortably while it's busy in its endless expression. It is not entirely up to us to choose our destiny, but we can choose to walk gracefully following the path laid out for us.."

"Ah! Guru-Ma is cooking again!" he interrupted himself, as he inhaled the fragrance of warm ghee, milk and rice that flowed from his kitchen. "Can you imagine my frustration in trying to be mindful of the portions I consume?" he asked, laughing at his own words as Sita joined in.

They had made it home. Valmiki let go of Sita's hand and slowly stepped inside. Sita, unhesitatingly and with great comfort, walked into the kitchen. When she asked Guru-Ma to step aside, the older woman did so with a smile. Today Sita would prepare breakfast for her foster parents.

There are very few of us who have that within us, which evokes comfort in others, Sita noticed the love she felt for Guru-Ma and Valmiki as she stirred the pot that was filled with spiced rice and lentils. Their home had been her temple where she had felt safe and loved whatever the nature of her thoughts or feelings on any given day. Here she had experienced the rare suspension of judgment and calculation. This relationship had been a blessing like none other she had known. This home radiated such great warmth that it invoked piety in all who visited. It was a place that threw light upon one's humaneness, gave a kindly embrace extending to the limits of one's personality. In the end, even with all of one's vulnerability exposed, one felt loved and cared for in this home.

Sita served Valmiki and Guru-Ma, who relished their humble meal and savored every bite with appreciation. Fanning them gently as they ate, Sita felt grateful that she was able to care for them. Since their home provided little respite from the hot, blazing sun, the aged couple rejoiced in the breeze of the fan, the fresh fruit that Sita cut for them and the cold water she offered. They each experienced great gratitude.

After they had finished eating, Sita said gently, "I think the time has arrived for young Lava and Kusha to meet their father. They are destined to be rulers, and I cannot erase their fate. I would like to send word to King Rama informing him of the preparedness of his children. After which I shall leave matters in the hands of destiny."

As she spoke, tears welled up in her large eyes. Guru-Ma moved closer and held her warmly; Valmiki waited in patience for the young mother to fully experience the grief of this anticipated change in her life.

"Are you willing to part with your children? Are you ready for this, Sita?" Valmiki inquired.

"No, I am not, and perhaps I will never be completely ready. But their place is not within the safety of this hermitage. They are destined for greatness. They are destined to lead the generation-to-come with greater care and intuitiveness. They are here to redirect people's fear towards faith in the purpose of the universe. They are here to bring new vision and enlightenment. They already have a task that is formidable and challenging, even though they collectively have the strength for it. It is time for me to empower my children and not stand in their way. I can imagine the agony my poor heart will be subjected to, once more, and I hate what is to come. But I have provided them with roots and now I need to encourage them to wear their wings."

Tears rolled down Valmiki's face. "I will send word to King Rama and visit him soon, my dear. Let me see for myself if he is willing to accept the twins and help them in furthering their interests."

Outside, the students had begun their morning prayer. The children, neatly dressed and prepared, chanted the Gayathri mantra in unison.

ॐ भूर्भुवः स्वः।
तत्सवितुर्वरेण्यं ।
भर्गो देवस्य धीमहि ।
धियो यो नः प्रचोदयात् ॥

Aum bhūr bhuvah svah |
tátsavitúr váren(i)yam |
bhárgo devásya dhīmahi |
dhíyo yó nah pracodáyāt ||

"I pray to the mother who resides in all of time, in the realm of our experience and in each of our human attributes. I ask of you to shine upon my intellect and dispel my ignorance. Just as the splendid sunlight dispels all darkness, I ask of you to make my intellect serene and bright."

XVI.

WIDOW'S OUTBURST

Meanwhile, back in Ayodhya, Rama had spent another sleepless night lying awake on his floor-mattress. He was in deep distress! He heard the early morning song of the lark hidden in a nest in the poplar tree – a song that mingled with the rhythmic hymns chanted by the temple priests, accompanied by ringing bells and the sound of conches.

The city was awakening, duty beckoned. The King knew he should rise, but his heart felt all too heavy, and so he lay still, unable to understand the thoughts that crossed his mind, numbed by the incomprehensible sadness that had come upon him.

The orange rays of the sun pried open the sleepy eyelids of the cool blue sky, demanding that Rama be ready for the reception of visitors. Rama's servants entered his chambers and stood in silence against the walls. The day had begun; it waited for no king and no God.

Struggling to get out of bed, Rama, tried to willfully crush his own reluctance as he stepped on the cold chamber floor. As seen in the mirror that hung on the wall across from the balcony, his scantily furnished chamber was juxtaposed to the immaculate palatial gardens. The tall ceilings of his chamber were decorated with paintings; reliefs were etched along the border of the walls. Gold plated chandeliers were fastened to the walls made of stone and silk drapes dressed the windows in the corridor. Once, his bedroom had been exquisitely furnished; now it was nothing more than a vacant-looking space.

Like the abundance of emotions that ebbed and flowed – whether or not there was the smallest change in the reality of his circumstance – Rama looked ahead to a day strung with events and rituals that did not draw-in his heart. Having chosen his own suffering, Rama had taken to sleeping on the floor. Having given up his kingly attire, he dressed in simple clothes. His meals were humble. Everything was lacking in royal extravagance of any kind.

Twelve years had gone by since he had ordered Sita to be abandoned in the forest! His once luxuriant black hair was now streaked with silver. His face was still beautiful, with its attractive features intact, but there were dark circles etched around his eyes. Though his body stood straight and tall, his shoulders were rounded. A certain sadness that almost felt ancient had settled into his heart. Victories over enemies, the enlargement of empire, successful governance, recognition and respect from his people, adulation, and wealth – all of this had come easily to him. He'd had it all, and still he was unfulfilled. The quest was never really satiated, and his soul remained hungry no matter what.

Learned men, scholars, philosophers, sages and priests surrounded Rama, and yet not one of them could grant him the peace he longed for. He was in control of a strong and powerful army, which was well trained and well equipped. There remained no enemies who dared to oppose the mighty King, and Ayodhya prospered under his rule.

Unlike his father, Rama actively participated in the day-to-day governance of his empire, imparting justice, formulating laws, encouraging learning, providing patronage to artists, establishing educational institutions, and participating in the celebrations of his people – all were part of his routine. And yet, at nighttime, in the dense darkness of his cool chambers, he struggled with his own demons.

The memory of Sita troubled him. He was haunted by his decision to send her away; the loss of her companionship had dried out his appetite for life. That she had been banished because of his sense of impropriety – his feeling of justified righteousness – rendered him hollowed out. Each morning he ran to his work and ran away from Sita's memory.

His pain had grown a scab prematurely upon the unhealed wound, and his unexpressed grief festered within him, hidden by his fear. In his mind, his hands remained tied; in his mind, his decision was irreversible, he was but a helpless executioner. His mind had authoritatively booked his emotions as feeble, and yet his mind remained restless. Even when, on occasion, he mustered the courage to settle his restless mind, he simply did not know how to do so.

The seed of righteousness had been planted in him as a young boy, and from that seed had grown a strong, overbearing tree that ruled his heart with infinite criticism. He wanted fairness in his compassion, reciprocation in his love, clarity in his fear, and justification in his happiness! If only the human mind could over-rule the human heart without consequence.

As usual, Rama bathed, got dressed, and broke his fast with fruit that he barely tasted. He walked hurriedly toward the entourage that was waiting to take him to the court hall in the southwest corner of the city. Citizens waved, hailing him with praises as the chariots rolled across the broad cobblestone streets to the large rectangular building that was flanked by a steep set of stairs and two large reliefs of the rising sun, the symbol of the royal household.

The building itself was composed of a long hall with a ceiling supported on all sides by columns. At the eastern end of the building was a semi-circular elevation bearing a gold-plated throne, the seat of King Rama. Inside the building were two parallel aisles. Ministers and administrators who sat on cushions along each aisle participated in the proceedings whenever invited by their king.

The central open area, guarded by soldiers, was where common folk could present their matters before the court. Trumpets blew to announce the arrival of the King of Ayodhya. Rama heard a wave of cheers from his subjects, and his heaviness lifted a bit. With a great sense of relief, he took his place on the throne and gestured for the court to proceed.

The agenda presented before the court included matters that were fairly mundane – a dispute over a well, another dispute over rightful inheritance and a case of insubordination by a soldier and the non-observance of a treaty by a small warlord. The laws on these matters were strictly codified, and justice was handed out expeditiously as there was little room for interpretation.

It was almost midday before a new matter was finally presented before the court. The hot sun and thick humid air made the crowd lethargic, and a sense of tedium enveloped the court. Everyone seemed to be in haste to wind up matters and retire into the cool shade of the inner chambers of their homes. Yet Rama ordered the proceedings to continue; this would be the last case he would hear today.

A dispute had broken out between a widow and the brothers of her late husband. The brothers argued that the woman was impure and therefore could not be considered part of the family. They argued that she was unfit to inherit the property owned by her late husband, which she was to keep under her care as trustee for her under-aged son. The brothers of the deceased man argued that they were forced to intercede on behalf of the boy, as the woman could not be trusted.

The law supported the cause of the widow. It was clear that she was entitled to the rights that were being challenged. The matter required an exception based on the subjective analysis of her character, and this was fairly unusual. Rama observed that the brothers of the deceased man seemed confident of victory, and he was curious to know more. When he sought an explanation, they volunteered unhesitatingly.

"Supreme Master, we belong to a line of washer-men! Our dead brother was one himself. Several years back, this woman who calls herself his wife was abducted and molested by an enemy of our brother. She was forced to stay in his house for a whole week before she was released. Our brother refused to take her in at first, claiming that she was unclean, but due to reasons that remain a mystery to us he changed his mind a year later. We tried, but we could not convince our brother to refrain from bringing this impure, filthy woman back into our family once more. She produced a son after she was taken back. Now our brother, who we think was not of sound mind, is dead. We want to prevent this woman from having any further interaction with our nephew and we want to protect him. We will provide and care for our nephew until the boy comes of age. We would like to be appointed lawful guardians of him and the property our brother left behind. Though this unclean woman claims she was abducted and did not leave by her own will, there is no way we can be certain of that."

"Also, Master, gathering all of my courage I would like to bring to your attention that my brother was the washer-man whose words caused you – the Greatest of Great Kings, Supreme Ruler and Unchallenged hero of the whole world – to banish his Queen Sita from the palace. You have set the standard for piety in a woman. You understand the right way in which men should handle such matters. We therefore assume that there will be no hesitation from you to grant to us what we rightfully wish for."

The whole court fell silent.

Rama slowly turned his gaze towards the widow. She stood firmly in place, staring at him indignantly! Her eyes smoldered with rage, revealing her fearlessness, and her lips pressed against her teeth with restrained fury.

Suddenly she burst out at King Rama, "Yes! My husband was a better man than you will ever be, King Rama! His heart was larger and found compassion for me. Sure he was angry at the situation our family was needlessly dragged into by a lust-filled monster. But being unable to watch my helpless plight, he changed his mind and offered me his compassion. Our life together was anything but easy, yet the strength of our love made it wonderful. Even now, when he lies dead, I feel the power of his love tenderly holding this aching heart of mine. But I don't expect that you can comprehend any of this! How was it Sita's fault that the demon Ravana could not temper his lust with prudence? Why is it that she has to pay for the sins of the slain monster? That which is not given from the heart is received only in sin-filled oppression! Rich is the man who can hold a woman's heart with respectful tenderness! Oh! Great King, you could have set the path for honoring women by accepting your wife for the woman that she was – loving and kind. But by betraying her in her hour of need, you have betrayed centuries of women to come. Do as you please by me and my son, I fear not you or your lame judiciary."

Rama was rendered speechless by the force of her words.

Without warning his supressed pain broke its barriers and came gushing into his heart, flooding him with feelings of intolerable agony. Blood drained from his face, and his hands and feet went cold. He turned away from the court in a failed attempt to hide the tears that streamed from his pain-filled eyes. His will to resist this abrupt interruption was crushed by the strength of the unexpressed grief buried within him.

Sadly, Rama's attempt to gain composure was rewarded only with greater fury of his unbridled grief. Needless to say, he submitted to it! Of what purpose were all his knowledge and his accomplishments when he had simply lacked the compassion to do what a common illiterate washerman had done? It was obvious that the lives of this ordinary couple had been far from easy. They had been subject to ridicule from family, had suffered isolation from their community and consistent public humiliation. And yet they had survived! They had made a life for themselves based upon their mutual love. Oh! How poor was his own love for his beloved Sita, compared to the kind of love this common man possessed for his wife!

Why had he, the great King Rama, punished the victim? He had lacked vision in his judgment! He had erred in favor of pride-filled men. and he had strangled the voice of women. He had failed!

The court was shocked to see their King melt down in this unforeseen torment. An uncomfortable silence prevailed at the sight of this unprecedented display of feelings. To display such emotions was simply not the prerogative of Kings and rulers! In the gathering, men glanced awkwardly at each other; helplessly unaware of what precedent they should follow. They had expected that their king would be infuriated by the words of this wretched woman. They had hoped he would silence her the moment she had begun. After all, no woman had ever before dared to address a King so very brutally! And yet! She spoke rightly from her heart!

A good majority of the men in the crowd were tired. Their fatigue at the prevalent culture rendered them helpless as they watched their beloved sisters and daughters being treated with disrespect and unkindness. But centuries of custom and age-old traditions were being followed and, as men, they had to make sure that these rules of society were maintained. Or at least that was what they believed! Lawlessness threatened their existence! Change made them anxious! Yet their refusal to change made them primitive and uncultured in their practice. They needed leadership that they could trust, one who could guide them. These women needed the help and support of men to correct the imbalance. And yet they feared suggesting it to their king and emperor.

King Rama struggled to gain his poise. With a gesture, he asked everyone to leave, a plea they obeyed in silence. As they dispersed, many felt the pain-filled sacrifice made by their beloved king; their hearts ached, but they were unsure of how to express these unmanly emotions. A few smirked at each other, as if conveying their distaste at such a display as the king had shown. A few more felt too great a shame and could not look one another in the eye. Anxiety gripped the court and the kingdom!

"Oh, Sita, what have I done?" Rama whispered as he broke down and wept.

So many tears had remained unshed, and now they flowed endlessly. Tears marked as weakness and stowed away, tears filled with sadness and suppressed, tears that had been buried alive in his body and tormented by his mind night after night – all found release.

Thus he grieved, this human king who, having rejected his humanity, was suffocating within himself. Today his heart could not hold his overflowing grief any longer, and his mind had lost its resourcefulness. But his soul was finally set free!

XVII.

VALMIKI IN AYODHYA

The thick labyrinth of broad roads and narrow walkways leading to the city of Ayodhya, the capital of the empire, merged at the heavily guarded gateways to the city. Tall columns of massive stone and mortar were linked by magnificent semi-circular arches; travelers looked up at these gateways with awe. Near the city were numerous guards on patrol, dressed in bright red and orange garments, armed with glittering swords.

The roads were packed with everyday travelers, traders on horses, ox-driven carriages filled with grain, herdsmen with cattle, and hunters with dried meats – all on their way to the city's enormous markets. Weary from traveling all day, approaching the city with his entourage of disciples upon horseback, Valmiki was astonished at the sight of Ayodhya.

The mid-morning air was heavy with the indescribable scent produced by so many people and animals living in close quarters. Valmiki smelled prepared foods, spices, flowers, fruits, hay for cattle, dust from the hoofs of horses, and cattle dung, all mixed with the pungent odor of drainage water from the city. A variety of traders from far-off kingdoms in colorful, unfamiliar costumes attracted the attention of the guards.

Valmiki stopped for a moment, taking in the sights of the well-planned city. Narrow, earth-caked lanes led to stone-paved broad streets filled with horses, carts, and people. These lanes were flanked by flat-roofed brick houses with mud-caked walls of varied colors, standing in bright contrast against the endless blues of the sky.

Valmiki heard languages he had never known to exist as he observed traders from far-away countries. The temptation of new and interesting experiences filled his aged limbs with new energy and encouraged him to continue patiently along the path.

But suddenly he stopped – overwhelmed by excitement. Filled with curiosity, he realized he was being carried away from his real purpose. With a smile on his face, he reminded himself once again of his intention! He was there in Ayodhya to have a conversation with King Rama about his estranged sons Lava and Kusha!

But again he was distracted—this time by the sight of camel, dressed in bright colors, with an embroidered rug thrown across its back, bells tied around its neck, and painted hoofs. He strove to bring back his attention back to his purpose, but it was like a mother disciplining a wayward child. Inwardly, he pleaded with himself to give up its childlike behavior for a moment. Then, as if realizing that he was too old to care, he gave in and let his attention wander, allowing himself his indulgences.

A stunningly dressed officer who was waiting at the palace gates in his horse-driven chariot stepped down and approached Valmiki. The palace had been informed a few weeks earlier that the enlightened one was planning a visit to the city of Ayodhya. Valmiki's disciple, dressed in a dhoti and plain white shirt, stepped forward and announced the great sage to the officer, who then bowed to Valmiki and directed the entourage to follow him into the palace. Crowds at the city gate were ordered to step aside and make way for this sage who, they saw, was to be received with great honor.

Unaccustomed to pomp and show, Valmiki smiled nervously at the crowds. Dressed in simple white clothing – with his long, white, flowing beard and hair tied back in a tuft – the enlightened sage stepped into Ayodhya in his wooden slippers as the crowds bowed down in reverence!

Life within the city filled Valmiki with wonder and a feeling of adventure. The sound of his horses' hooves seemed to reverberate in rhythm with the hidden songs of the city streets. He passed the citizens' brick houses, packed closely together, and observed their wooden doors and windows. Most homes had inner courtyards with outer walls that opened up into the roadside. Narrow lanes broadened out into wide-open spaces containing enormous markets filled with vendors of, spices, fruits, trinkets, vegetables, clothing, housewares, domesticated animals, and flowers. The welcoming shouts of eager salesmen, the bargaining of the hopeful, the laughter and games of children, and the color-dyed saris of the women stimulated the senses. He noticed, with sympathy, the conversation being held between a father and his young son who seemed to be trying to determine the object to purchase before entering a store that held many temptations. Here and there sat aged citizens enjoying games of dice under the shade of trees as they fervently discussed prices, crops, and weather. A snake charmer had caught the attention of several wayfarers as he charmed a shiny black cobra out of its cramped wicker basket and prompted it to dance to the hypnotic music of his pipe. Dressed in a bright, multi-colored turban and sporting a bushy mustache with long sideburns, the snake charmer's risky entertainment produced wonder in curious onlookers and earned him many coins.

A wedding party crossed the street, making its way to the temple in the far corner. Men and women dressed in bright-hued costumes danced around the groom riding his white horse, accompanied by a flourishing band of blaring trumpets and beating drums.

The temple, with its immaculate stone carvings and its lofty conical head, sported a shiny brass gate. An elephant stood by the corner, along with the mahout offering blessings by placing its trunk upon the heads of pilgrims in return for gifts of fruit and flowers. At every other corner were wells where sari-clad women drew water and filled large pots they carried back home, chatting and laughing. Huge, mud-brick mounds housed centrally located baths that had areas cordoned off for different genders. Weavers were creating intricately patterned fabric; potters worked clay pots that had geometric engravings; goldsmiths displayed their exquisite jewelry; and coppersmiths offered their newly made pots and utensils – just some of the many craftsmen with shops lining the streets. Observing residents bustling back and forth in haste, for a few moments Valmiki felt his own life entangled in the whirl of the busy city.

Just as they turned a corner, seemingly out of no-where there appeared a massive earthen moat surrounding a stone fortress with tall, thick outer walls and circular bastions. The walls of this fortress extended as far as the eye could see. Within the walls of these huge blocks of stone were housed high-ranking officials, government officers, and the royal family. The moat surrounding this intimidating structure was spanned by wooden ramps that could be raised or lowered to control access.

On the far side of the ramps were enormous, wooden double doors strengthened with strong iron beams. Opening those doors required a team of fifteen soldiers who were posted there. The sage and his entourage proceeded into this colossal fortress with equal measures of awe and apprehension.

Once inside, Valmiki was struck by what he saw. Four large roads led in the four cardinal directions with a temple to the God Vishnu situated in the center. The wealth of the king, whose opulent home was in the northern corner of the fortress, was strikingly apparent. The fortress also housed several other palatial homes with elaborate gardens, pavilions, manicured lawns, fountains, fruit orchards, horse stables (with the finest of horses), formidable stables for elephants, and stands for chariots. Armed guards watched over every nook and cranny of this fortress.

The party was led to the guest quarters where they were to rest and refresh themselves. The King would provide them the audience that the sage sought, just as soon as Valmiki felt ready.

Valmiki, tired from travelling for an entire day on horseback, was treated to a warm, perfumed bath, then given brand new robes and offered a delight of dishes prepared to perfection. When he lay down for his night's rest, however, he shunned the silk bed with its enormous cushions and slept instead on the earth as he had always done at the hermitage. He slept peacefully.

The following morning, Valmiki rose before daybreak and sat wondering about his austere life back in the hermitage. He felt tremendous gratitude for the life that he had created for himself – a life filled with simplicity and the subtle joys of living, unencumbered by material consumption and constant worry about the imagined future, unlike those forever preparing for a moment not in the present. For the first time, he realized the luxuries that Sita had been forced to cut out of her life when she had entered his hermitage. He felt love and admiration for the young woman who had received, with great humility and gratitude, the meager offerings of his hermitage.

Not far away from Valmiki, King Rama lay awake wondering about the reason for Valmiki's visit to his palace. He was not ignorant of Sita's presence or of the birth of his twin sons in Valimiki's hermitage. His vast spy network had kept him informed of everything that transpired in his kingdom.

Rama felt immense gratitude towards this humble sage who had given refuge to Sita and protected her – when he, despite all his power and wealth, had been unable to do so. He had been taken by surprise when one of Valmiki's trusted disciples had shown up at the palace and informed him of the sage's desire to visit Ayodhya. Rama's heart had leapt with joy, though that quickly changed to apprehension. He had however granted the wise sage the audience he desired.

The turn of events with the washer-man's widow had left Rama unhinged, feeling uncertain about everything. His idealistic pursuit of time-tested values had failed him, leaving him without faith in the established system. The fact that he had endured self-imposed hardships similar to those of his estranged wife did not make up for the fact that he had not acted rightly by her or by himself. In the end, the washer-man who had a change of heart and had gracefully taken his wife back, had enjoyed a much more fulfilled life than this great King. Rama had appeased the ego and ignored his soul.

Since the day of the unfortunate incident at the court hall, Rama had withdrawn from his duties and shut himself off in his chamber. A weight of unbearable pain crushed him remorselessly. He felt himself sinking into an abyss of existence, too weak to offer prayers and plead with the Gods. He could not bring himself to attempt to hold on, even to the crumbling soil along the edges. Instead, he had given in and allowed himself to fall! Sleep and appetite were the first to go, followed by meaning and hope! Even subtle joys – such as the smile of a child or the song of a wee bird – did not even remotely stir a need to react! He lay as if dead, awaiting his final hour, too apathetic to even reach out to death that was within a hand's distance, lying motionless as it crawled closer without flinching.

Finally the hour came. Late in the morning, Sage Valmiki was led to the palatial quarters of the great King. Flowerbeds lined the walkway, and peacocks danced vibrantly in the meadows. The palace, set upon broad steps of polished stone, glittered in the warmth of the bright sun. Supported by large columns and huge arches, the wide passageway led to an atrium in the center of which was a pond with pale pink lotuses. The rooms that surrounded this portico were decorated with intricately carved furniture studded with gold and embroidered coverings. Historic paintings covered the walls. Everywhere within sight were extravagances that thrilled the senses. The doorman announced the arrival of the great sage as he entered the quarters of King Rama.

But Valmiki was shocked by the unexpectedness of what he saw: the inner chambers of the king stood in stark contrast to the riches of the palatial fort!

The large room, sporting a balcony that opened into the lawns, was completely austere. It smelled of pressed lavender hidden in the chests of the simple furniture that seemed dwarfed by high walls, as if fearful of distracting anyone. It was evident that King Rama, too, slept on the floor, as a thin mattress was spread out in the center of the room. The chamber echoed with the sound of sadness, desperation, and hurt.

The great King was dressed in simple white cottons, lacking any of the finery or striking jewelry customarily worn by royalty. His shoulder-length hair, curling at the nape of his neck, was brushed and held in place by the perfect contours of his ears. His forehead appeared wide and sculpted; beneath, well-defined eyebrows were shadowed deep brown eyes that were open and honest. An unspoken, long-standing grief was engraved in the corners of his mouth and in the expression of his eyes. This King in no way resembled the intimidating surroundings outside this chamber. To Valmiki, this King felt extraordinarily human.

Rama looked at Valmiki as he folded his hands and bent his head forward, indicating deep respect. Valmiki, too, repeated this simple act with humility and openness. However, when Valmiki lifted his head, he found that Rama's eyes were filled with tears that streamed down his cheeks. He seemed unable to lift his gaze and look into the eyes of the humble sage.

Instantly Valmiki's tender heart was filled with compassion for this suffering human. He stepped closer and placed his hand on Rama's shoulder. At that moment Rama gained control; he invited the revered sage to take a seat beside him on simple, low, wooden stools.

"I hope that your journey was pleasant and you are well rested, Sage Valmiki," said Rama politely.

"Yes, my journey was a pleasant one and I feel rested," Valmiki replied in a soft, unassuming voice.

Rama waited, assuming that Valmiki would continue; instead Valmiki just gazed into Rama's tear-filled eyes. The silence between the two men made Rama immensely uncomfortable, and he searched his mind for some topic of conversation that would be relevant.

After a few more moments Valmiki spoke softly, "Please tell me, dear King, why were there tears in your eyes today? I have a reason for my visit, but I would like to hear your story first, if you would be so kind as to share it with me."

Rama hesitated before answering in a voice filled with pain and sorrow, "I feel lost, great sage! The ground I stand on does not feel firm anymore! I feel like I have erred greatly and acted hastily, in driving my dear and pregnant wife out of the empire and into the forest. I am aware of your kindness towards Sita and her twin sons, and am deeply grateful for it."

Noticing Valmiki's lack of surprise as he made this statement, Rama continued. "I thought that it was the right thing to do! I thought that by following the right path, I was setting a good example. I thought there is such a thing as a right path that holds true in all situations. It turns out I have caused Sita to suffer needlessly, and I have suffered senselessly as well. My life, my beliefs, and my ideals have failed to give me the peace I desire! I have withheld myself from the affections of my wife and my children who are strangers to me now. I cannot seem to find my way back into this world!"

Rama stopped and exhaled. His voice was filled with agony, his handsome face filled with horror. The sound of peacocks crowing drifted toward this spartan chamber, but it was a sound that seemed to be arrested upon entering. In fact it seemed as if this chamber curtailed the entry of any joy or laughter that might have entertained the king. Rama, oblivious to his surroundings, continued on with his talk.

"I was blinded by my ideals! When an ordinary citizen disowned his wife who had suffered a plight similar to that of Sita, I assumed incorrectly that Sita was not the cherished example to women in my empire, and I disowned her ungraciously. Unable to garner the strength to explain my reasons, it was cowardly of me to have my brother take her into the forest and abandon her. He was powerless in trying to dissuade me from my impulsivity. Lakshmana, my brother, thoughtfully left her close to your hermitage knowing that she would be protected. Had it not been for your compassionate caring, she would have never survived in that wild forest.

"Recently the washer-man's wife, now a widow, came to my court. She laughed with contempt at my assumed righteousness and elaborated on how her illiterate husband had more heart and was a better person than I. With his kindness he had gained back her love and enjoyed the affection of their child to the very last day of his life. She asked me if I had earned anything that would stay with me until my very last breath. I realized I have nothing!"

"I have punished my heart by driving away what was most precious to me – Sita! She was the only one who understood me, not as a prince or a husband but as a human – a human with hopes, fears, aspirations, and struggles. And I let her go – the only person who shone a light upon my soul! I have been walking around empty and soulless ever since. Filled with the arrogance of my righteousness and fearing reflection, I have pursued all the shadows of existence, wealth, fame, renown, and respect – all of which have left me unfulfilled. I have forgotten what it is like to be loved!"

Rama's voice cracked with sorrow. He paused, unable to speak further.

Tears streamed from Valmiki's eyes. He sat in silence beside the king. Rama was no longer blinded by ignorance. He was aware of his grief, aware of the pain in his heart, aware of the injury and suffering he had caused. Words were redundant. This King was no longer living unconsciously; awareness had stepped into his life and brought forth the truth for him to see. This awareness would provide the cure to his grieving heart and restore his spirit. All Rama needed at the moment was a compassionate companion to sit beside him for as long as it would take for his spirit to recover.

Rama turned to look at Valmiki and asked gently, "Kind sage, what brings you to this city? I dare not ask you about my wife and children as I feel undeserving of even speaking their names. Please forgive me!"

Valmiki spoke without hesitation, "They are well, dear Rama. The boys and Sita are all happy back at the hermitage. Sita has become indispensable to the residents of our hermitage; she is a wise teacher and sets an extraordinary example for the women there. Lava and Kusha, your twin sons, have grown into loving, caring, and compassionate young men. Lava, your firstborn, is a fine warrior who will excel in his chosen field. Kusha – the younger of the two – is filled with wisdom beyond his years. We have provided the boys with all the knowledge and learning that can be had while they are living in the hermitage. But they yearn for far more, and their destiny is not to live shielded by the protective environment there. The children have to face the larger world and seem eager to do so. Here in Ayodhya, the boys can be trained further and refine their skills. Are you willing to give Lava and Kusha what is rightfully theirs, dear Rama?"

Rama was struck by these words. The prospect of being engaged in the life of his children in any way had seemed remote just a moment ago. And yet he was sure the sage Valmiki mentioned Lava, Kusha, and Ayodhya all in the same string of words. His heart grasped at this fortuitous opportunity!

Rama replied unhesitatingly, "Lava and Kusha – beautiful names! Yes! My children should certainly get everything that I inherited from my ancestors. I will give them that, great sage! But do they... Oh! Great one... do they know of me as their father? Is Sita willing to send the boys to Ayodhya? Will they be willing to forgive me for my thoughtless deeds? I feel great apprehension and fear at the prospect of meeting them, and yet nothing in this world can make me happier!"

Valmiki smiled as he replied, "It is a brand new beginning for sure, and fear is to be anticipated. Both yours and theirs! You will have to wait and discover if forgiveness is possible, dear Rama. Please keep an open heart and love them for who they are, without any expectation.

I will repeat what my wife said to me when I asked for her forgiveness years ago, Guru-Ma wisely told me that only I can forgive myself. Treat yourself with kindness, great King. There is not one amongst us who has not erred. Courageous are those who accept the truths of their life with a compassionate heart."

Rama's heart lifted as he heard these kind words. He felt a wave of relief drift into his body, while his restless mind calmed down and stopped its chatter for a moment. He held Valmiki's hands in his, and thanked him once again!

Soon, plans for the king to leave for the hermitage would be made with great enthusiasm.

XVIII.

RETURN

Three days after Sage Valmiki arrived in Ayodhya, King Rama briefed selective members of his administration and his loyal brother Lakshmana about his intention to leave the capital for a few days.

Leaving behind his crown, the ring bearing the image of the rising sun, the ceremonial mace, and casting aside his sword with its royal insignia, Rama hurriedly got ready to leave the city. He dressed himself as a commoner in a white dhoti, a robe that fell loosely upon his left shoulder, and wore a turban. Rama left his palace in the wee hours of the morning, accompanied by Valmiki, beginning their long journey back to the hermitage.

As they passed through the gates of the city, they went unrecognized by the guards, who mistook them for regular travelers and simply ushered them over to the other side of the moat. They smiled at each other; their plan had worked without a flaw. The entourage of disciples accompanying the sage had previously departed from the city, and now they waited at the end of the road, their horses saddled for their dear teacher and his new companion.

Apart from a trusted few, the vast majority of the population had been informed that Valmiki had remained in the palace and King Rama was receiving his guidance.

It had been a very long time since Rama's heart had felt enthusiastic as he stepped upon the bare earth. Now, as he strode the narrow path fringed with soft wet grass – without trumpets, guards, mace holders or cheering audience – Rama felt human. The powdery crust of the red earth stained his feet and his lungs were filled with crisp morning air. A childlike happiness, though vague and still shy, entered into him as he discovered within himself the anticipation of an adventure! The sight of the sun rising high in the eastern sky seemed to arouse a rainbow of warm feelings within his shriveled heart.

Valmiki felt delighted to see his disciples and embraced each of them warmly in appreciation for their dedication. The presence of the elderly sage made the journey all the more interesting for King Rama.

Unhindered by the formalities of their respective stations, the two men conversed extensively as they rode down the winding pathways leading to the hermitage. Valmiki recollected with humor the deep fear he had experienced when, years before, he had decided to return to the family he had once abandoned.

And now he confided in Rama, "Believe me, I was certain that my hot-headed wife would slip a sharp blade into my core when I returned to her. It turned out that everything I had gone looking for, she had found right where she stood, in her tiny home, in the midst of caring for three young children. I felt so very humbled. I had to wait in patience for her to accept me once more! But it was worth it!"

Rama commented, "You know, kind Valmiki, the question that has haunted me all my life is whether I am worthy of love. Am I acceptable? What is the best course of action I can follow in order to earn the approval of those around me? I have wondered about this time and again! As I became more self-aware, the fear of rejection felt greater and went deeper! What if people knew of my innermost thoughts, my fears, my weaknesses, and my desires? What if people knew me – not in a way that they want to see me – but in the way I perceive myself? Would they love me despite all my glaring faults?"

Valmiki looked intently at Rama as he said, "Look around you, Rama, look at all the nature around you! Nature is not conscious of itself, neither is it perfect. But there is great beauty in its imperfection. We humans, on the other hand, live in fear of revealing our essential natures. So deep-rooted is the fear that we will not be accepted, that we hide our natures from our own selves, choosing to live unconsciously, confirming with conventions that we know not why we follow. The question that haunts you is age-old!"

He continued after a brief pause, "I am yet to come across a mother who does not think her child is perfect and deserving of love. Be that mother to yourself! Hold that which is imperfect in you with kindness. It takes great courage to reveal your true nature for everyone to see. But imagine the liberation you will feel when you finally drop the mask and allow your hidden self to shine upon this earth. That is the courage that I see in Sita."

Rama smiled on hearing Sita's name spoken with such pride and endearment. He turned to question Valmiki once again, "But conventions are created to be of use to society is it not revered sage? Wouldn't lawlessness prevail if there were no conventions? Can we live in a society as individuals?"

Rama's face reflected his doubt.

Valmiki looked at Rama in surprise and asked, "Why not? Why can we not live as respectful individuals within a society? What is this fear about? Is it the fear of change? Is it the anxiety of having to venture out into the unknown and find a new path? It is! Is it not? It is fear of change and the anxiety that comes along with it. Then, dear king, who is setting the precedence here, is it your wisdom or is it your fear and anxiety? Whom do you wish to rule over – you, your wisdom, or your fear?"

Valmiki's response was so full of vigor and passion that Rama was taken aback. It was clear he had acted out of fear and anxiety when he had banished Sita from the kingdom. Yet he had taken refuge in unexamined convention and acted without employing wisdom. Valmiki was quick to notice how Rama's face fell.

Valmiki spoke more softly this time. "Dear Rama, conventions have always been established for the good of everyone. Offering protection to women, children, the aged, the sick, the invalid, and the vulnerable with respect and compassion is the purpose of convention. Yet just as everything is changing moment by moment, society is changing too. Change makes people nervous, as the outcome of changing situations cannot be foretold or predicted. By refusing to release the grip on established convention, we fool ourselves into believing that we are being just and lawful when in reality we are being fearful and anxious. We require wise and courageous leadership in order to assure people that new ways will be welcome. We require dauntless guidance from our leaders to experiment with newness – to have the nerve to accept failure just as humbly as one would adorn successes. Rama, while your mind may dwell on the gravity of your errors, I see enormous courage in you, in your willingness to recognize and accept your limitations. Your awareness is the first step towards conscious living. Have faith, my dear Rama. Be open and accepting of the experiences life blesses you with."

Rama exhaled softly. His heart and mind traveled to the memory of his dear and beloved wife Sita. Anxiety brewed slowly and flitted within his chest.

"Where did it go wrong? My marriage! I adored her so very deeply!" he whispered. The question lingered in the air as if it would hang there until answered.

Rama continued, "We were young, innocent, enthusiastic and so deeply in love! The love we possessed for each other it brought us such great joy and fulfillment. I wonder if there was a fault in our love that we have hurt each other so very deeply? What has married life been like for you, great sage?"

Rama surprised himself, speaking so freely and from the heart!

Valmiki thought for a minute before he replied, "It's the nature of love! I jumped into marriage with Guru-Ma simply because she made me happy! It was an addiction, the quality of love that we initially experienced. It made us both feel happy and fulfilled, borrowing heavily and being dependent on each other. We had both completely ignored that fact that deep down we are all always alone. Rama, no matter how close you get to another human, there is always a piece of you that remains isolated, unknown, and unknowable to another. Uncomfortable with the aloneness that we experience deep within, we grasp and hold on to each other in the hope of getting away from it. All our momentary fulfillments – be they physical intimacy or light-hearted companionship – we label as our happiness and struggle as these fulfillments leave us every time. We think it should last forever. It was only when I ran into the seven sages in the forest that I realized that true peace meant to be comfortable with the aloneness that I ran from. It was inevitable. I had to leave home to find myself. It is the only way available for a man."

"After years of penance and following false leads, one fine day I found this lasting peace! It too, lasted for a moment but its imprint remained upon me for the rest of my life! Fatigued and frustrated with penance and physical deprivation, one day I sat on a hill in the forest, weeping at my failure. Not knowing what path to assume, I stared at my surroundings. From the top of the hill, I could see valleys, tall trees, lakes, and I could hear a variety of birds. My mind quieted, I closed my eyes, and I heard myself saying, "They are all alive! And I am alive in it, too!" Suddenly I felt assimilated into the landscape around me; it was a strong sense of dissolution, like I could not differentiate between my life and the life around me. At that moment I realized that I was never alone, even when I thought and felt alone. A deep sense of comfort flooded my body and I felt at peace!"

Valmiki stopped in his path. He pointed at the shelter for travelers and asked, "Do you mind if we rest here for a bit?"

"Not at all, great sage!" replied Rama.

The entourage stopped at the rest area. Rama noted with great pleasure that he had succeeded in his effort to establish these rest spots all over the kingdom. The horses were unsaddled, given water and fresh hay. The men ate bread that was baked in a clay oven and served with spiced vegetables. They rested on the cool grass under shade of the trees and conversed with fellow travelers about their trade and travels. Rama sat by Valmiki, hoping he would continue his story – and indeed he did.

"Rama, there is not much to be done after you have attained enlightenment! Like all other states of being, the state of peaceful sublimation is also something that comes and goes! Surely your worldview is changed forever, but one does not get to reside in that state for eternity! You still feel hungry, thirsty, need love and love others. So I chose to go back to my family, hoping that Guru-Ma would take me in! I noticed how Guru-Ma no longer clamored or grasped at me either. She was not aloof or uncaring by any means, she was much more loving and kind. But there was a difference. It was that her identity and sense of self were no longer borrowed, that she had formulated a self that was different from me. As a man, I could offer her companionship and love, but she was no longer needy. She had gathered enough resources to find fulfillment and purpose. I felt way more attracted to her than I had ever been. I had hurt her, and it took a while to earn her faith back, but this time our love was different. This time it felt like two 'whole' beings were coming together. Sure, we loved each other's companionship, and our intimacy felt far deeper than ever before, but our relationship felt devoid of fear. We both knew that when we were together we would be together in love, and if we ever parted once again, we would part in love. Ah! It feels delicious to be loved as such!"

And then he added, with a laugh, "But not as delicious as her rice pudding – which I hope she will make for me soon!" With those final words, he settled down for a nap on the bare earth under the shade of a sprawling peepal tree.

Rama felt mesmerized by Valmiki's tale. He noticed how his heart had begun to feel more and more peaceful. He tasted each drop of water that he drank and every morsel of the simple food he shared with his fellow travelers. He heard everything – the laughter of young children, the singing of women by the riverbanks, the flute played by the cowherd, the ringing bells in the distant temples, and his own breath that inhaled and exuded life in all directions. His face was soft, the worry lines on his forehead had melted, and his eyes smiled once again. A part of him was envious of Valmiki – he so badly longed to experience the sense of safety that the great sage spoke about – and yet he knew he had to be patient.

They continued their journey after Valmiki's brief mid-day nap, hoping to make it to the banks of the river Tamasa by nightfall.

As they journeyed, curious Rama asked Valmiki once again, "Kind sage, you spoke of aloneness, is it the same as loneliness? At times I feel lonely even when I am in a crowd. Is that aloneness? Would you kindly explain that to me?" Rama's voice was filled with curiosity.

Valmiki pulled at the reins of his brown mare, and she halted abruptly, shuffling and snorting. The sage looked far into the distance for a few moments; then closed his eyes. When he opened them again, his eyes had a strange, luminous quality that Rama had not observed previously.

Valmiki spoke softly, "Rama, a cup filled with water comes together as particles of water filled in a cup. Rice pudding comes together as individual grains of rice cooked together in a pot. The field out there is composed of individual crops. This beautiful land on which we walk is made up of rivers, mountains, plains, and valleys. The plants grow, the trees die, the animals feed on each other, the fertile soil sprouts sapling from seeds, oceans retreat during low tides, rivers flood the plains, rock is rendered soft by slow-moving water, mothers give birth to children bringing together families, and we call all of this life. But it is also a summation of individual components, each having a definitive purpose. Deep down we are all one among the many tiny components that bring life together. We each have a peculiarity that is unique to our own self, and it is this quality that makes us alone. Loneliness comes and goes but aloneness stays forever!"

He studied Rama's face before he continued. "We fear our aloneness because recognizing it makes us feel separated from the whole, like an infant snatched from her mother. We avoid admitting it because of the discomfort that it brings us. We imitate those around us and follow others blindly hoping that we can save ourselves from parting from the whole. But water cannot be wind, which cannot be flower, which cannot become a seed. When we are in love we forget who we are and get engrossed in the other, and the feeling we experience is wonderful while it lasts. But this union cannot continue for long. Life demands that we be who we truly are. Life does not accept a seed that is unyielding, a bird that refuses to fly, or a fish that wishes to climb a tree. We need to be brave and courageous. As we get closer and closer to our true self, we become more and more fearful because we bring to the surface of our consciousness that which marks us as different from others. What has become revealed cannot be hidden any longer. Choices need to be made! But if you are to accept with an open heart what you have dared to find, it is at that moment you realize that you are you, and you are part of the whole. The love that comes with this finding, and acceptance of it, is universal and pervasive. For a seed to grow, sunshine, water, soil, and nutrients have to all come together. It is similar to the needs of each individual. The love that brings together two people that are aware of their inherent aloneness strengthens their sense of self. One does not attempt to swallow or suppress the other. This love creates space for each one to blossom in one's own way and it enables soulful expression. Such love is true love! Such love is the love of God!"

"But Rama, don't be fooled, we are but human! We learn, we forget, we learn once again, we forget what we learned once again. But practice brings us closer to perfection – yet perfection is impossible! So since we are only human, our love can only be real and not true. And real love has all the components of true love, along with fear, insecurity, neediness, and absorption. Awareness of your aloneness, awareness of the constant and persistent change in your internal landscape and acceptance of the thoughts, feelings and sensations that are visiting you can provide you with a sense of wellbeing. Wellbeing is not as intoxicating as being in love, but it is sustainable and makes allowance for errors."

Rama felt deeply satisfied on hearing this. Even when he noted, with a hint of self-criticism, the insatiability of his curiosity and his persistent questioning, he was tempted to learn more.

"If you do not mind answering this last question, dear Valmiki, I am curious to understand what made you go back to Guru-ma after you had found enlightenment," he asked, observing his own discomfort as the old sage gave him a broad smile.

"You have really built up your appetite Rama. And, sure, I would love to answer your question," said Valmiki, taking delight in the discomfort of his companion.

After taking a moment to compose himself once again, he resumed, "Realizing the importance and the inconsequence of my small and irrelevant self in the larger scheme of the universe did not make me disappear altogether, dear Rama! Enlightened or not, I still needed to care for my body, my mind, and my spirit for as long as I lived. I still needed to feed my body, bathe and dress myself, protect myself from the harsh elements, and teach others what I had experienced which I felt was the purpose of my being. But those others that I wished to teach – they weren't monks and sages, they were people in families who cared and lived for their families and communities. I did not know how to integrate my learning with everyday living – responsible living – living that requires care of others not just for one's own self."

Valmiki paused to note whether Rama comprehended his words. He smiled softly as he continued, "Well, Guru-Ma, had figured out what I struggled with! She had found peace in her heart while she cared for herself and the children, she had found compassion for her friends and neighbors, and she had found care for the young, the aging, and the vulnerable. I felt such great love and attraction towards the woman that she had become. I knew I had many more things I could learn from her. And I was determined to find a way into her heart, so my decision was easy. And sure enough, I was right in my reasoning."

He paused to make sure that he had the complete attention of his companion. This time he was not smiling.

In a voice that, though soft, bordered on reprimand, Valmiki continued, "It is the nurturing quality of a woman that keeps life together, just like mother earth. Her ability to give birth to life, and her innate desire to protect it blesses her with a softer and more amiable sense of self that is giving. Her love keeps life regenerating and nutritious. Does it not make sense that we men protect, empower, and provide loving care for our precious companions? Listen to her voice with care, King Rama. Provide her with encouragement to become her own person. You will be surprised at what she has to offer."

Valmiki stopped speaking, as if he had nothing more left to share. Rama felt great respect for this kind human. The hooves of their horses thudded on the soft earth. In the distance, the river Tamasa rumbled and roared. It would be dusk soon, and a few birds were already hurrying to fly home. The winding pathway opened up into plains along the banks of the river.

Suddenly, the horizon – previously hidden by the tree line – appeared at a distance. What the travelers saw was land that had been irrigated as far as the eye could see. Farmers with plows and oxen trudged through the wet soil after a long day of work. Rama felt himself melting into the landscape and was filled with a rare tranquility that could not be had at the palace. The hope of a happy reunion – one filled with tears, joy, and unlimited happiness – now filled his heart. And he admitted it inside – though nervously.

Valmiki yawned noisily as he remarked, "We should take a break from our journey right here on the banks of the river. We will be able to reach the hermitage, situated further south, by tomorrow afternoon if we get an early start in the morning."

The entourage of disciples hurried to follow the wishes of their teacher. Soon, makeshift tents were placed firmly into the ground, a huge fire was lit, and the horses, freed from their saddles, began to graze along the riverbanks. Valmiki washed himself in the river and sat down for his evening meditation. A few of the disciples scurried to prepare his evening meal, while others inquired whether the King was comfortable. Rama walked along the banks of the river and settled down upon a rock. His heart was at great peace at that moment.

The sky, a shade of darkening blue, spread out endlessly. The trees and shrubs on the bank exuded a strange comfort in their natural existence. Sitting by the riverbank, Rama drank in his surroundings with contentment. He was no longer a king, no longer a ruler, no longer son or brother, no longer husband and father. He was simply human. The stillness of his being gradually became integrated into the stillness of his surroundings. He felt assimilated into the flowing breeze, the grazing cattle, into the spaces between the leaves of the trees. He felt all his elements gathered together and scattered as fragments. It was as if he was the river that bounced against the rocks became the delicate flower growing unprotected, which transformed into the flutter of the birds, and marched along the footprints of an exhausted spider. His body felt ethereal and transparent, and his mind was absolutely still. How insignificant were his troubles and worries in comparison. Some strange sense of release freed his body, and his shoulders felt relaxed, and his limbs felt weightless and airy.

He walked back to the camp to enjoy the simple meal of rice and lentils offered by Valmiki's disciples. Valmiki had retired for the day and snored softly as he slept in his makeshift tent. The air was thick with the song of crickets. Rama found a spot beside the fire to lie down for the night. In the distance, a cow mooed into the darkness, and a faint voice could be heard singing a lullaby to a distressed infant. Rama gazed at the starlit sky and soon fell asleep.

✕

XIX.

DOUBTS AND ANXIETIES

Back in the hermitage, Lava turned in his bed once again. It was going to be a long night!

Aided by the hint of moonlight that stepped in shyly through the open window, Lava studied the profile of his brother, who was fast asleep. How did Kusha do so very well? He seemed gently embraced by the turns and twists of life, simply allowing them into the recesses of his tender soul.

It was not that Kusha was a coward unwilling to fight, but prudence seemed to be deeply embedded in him. He just absorbed, with ease and acceptance, the lessons given out by the great masters. Everyone who met him knew that he was destined for much greatness in his life. Lava felt deep love and admiration for him, along with a pang of envy.

He, Lava, was different from Kusha in a multitude of ways. Sure, he was a better archer than Kusha and all the other boys at the hermitage, but he was restless in his heart. What had been passed onto him as time-tested wisdom; he had to test out for himself before he would willingly accept it. Only that which made absolute sense did he embrace. He was, in a way, ferociously protective of those he loved; and he did not love timidly but with all his heart. Everything, and everyone, who had a place in his heart remained there forever. Emotions, in him, were imbued with his passionate energy, and there were times when he simply exploded. His anger and rage bore the same radiance as his love and compassion. He was born to protect. He rejoiced in caring for the elderly and the very young. It was not that he was disliked, but his constant questioning frustrated his teachers and other elders. And now he was unable to sleep as he wondered about this man who was his father.

Morning came at last, but a morning that opened its doors to the first day of spring. The many brooks that passed through the hermitage, tumbling from far-off mountains, seemed eager to announce the arrival of the season but found that they were late. Yellow rose buds standing among the soft sprouting grass smiled as if to say, "We already know!" A golden ray touched the front door of Sita's hut and danced so brightly that it was hard not to look away from the source.

The twin boys were up and out. They cleaned their teeth with an herbal concoction, spread onto the left palm, scooped up with the right index finger, and then applied to their teeth. They bathed at the falls where the stream shot past the rocks, seemingly intent on meeting the nearby river. They dressed, ate the morning meal that had been handed to them by their gracious mother, and were soon on their way to school.

Sita lingered by the door as she watched her handsome young children – cleaned, fed, and playful – walk down the curving path towards the open classroom. A dull ache caressed her heart and brought warm tears into her beautiful eyes at the thought of having to let go! They were children still, but not childlike anymore! No longer were they simply surrounded by people they called mother, teacher, friend, neighbor, priest, or farmer. For now they had begun to see the person behind the label. Therefore, the priest was no longer just a priest but an anxious man with a tendency to get their names confused; a friend was no longer just a friend but a boy who preferred riding a horse to memorizing the multiplication table. In all of this they had begun to look into their hearts and were surprised to find things there that were not identical. But even as they wove the delicate strings of their findings into the people they believed they were, they remained children, and like all children they liked definitive things that they could take and run with. They needed to know love, and they needed to identify hate – and Sita, as their mother, helped them know where their love should flow and what they could do with that hate.

The path to school was winding, and soon Lava and Kusha were out of sight. Sita stepped back into her hut with a sigh.

About the time Sage Valmiki had started his preparation to leave for Ayodhya, Sita had gathered her twin sons into her arms and whispered to them the purpose of Valmiki's visit. They had stared at her in surprise. She had looked each one of them in the eye as she informed them of her decision. Lava had held her tightly, a bit too tightly, and she had to pry his arms off her. Kusha had taken a step back but had returned to kiss her gently on her cheek. Sita knew there would be a lot more questions waiting for her at night, but she was surprised when the boys had gone about their business as usual. Awkwardness had stepped into her tightly knit family, and though she was tempted to take measures to erase the feeling, she had allowed it to stay, waiting for it to make its own way out. For such was her way of mothering her twin sons, in a manner which allowed them to see with their own eyes, feel with their own hearts, and allow them to make willful choices.

Just as soon as the two boys were out of the sight of their mother, Lava exploded, "I stayed up almost all of last night thinking!"

His words invited the curiosity of his twin.

"Do you not worry about leaving mother and this hermitage, Kusha?"

When Kusha remained silent, Lava continued, "I mean, don't you wonder about our father? Do you think he will be interested in anything that has to do with us? I don't know how I really feel about him! All this is confusing and scary! Not scary in the sense that I'm afraid, but simply because it makes me feel... shy. Not like a bride feeling shy – it's just that all of this is confusing, because I want to be the best archer and swordsman in the world, and I want to stay with you and Mother, and I don't want to leave the hermitage. But at the same time, I want to be trained by the best and I want for Mother to be happy, and I worry about our father the King. What if he hurts her or you, this father? What are we supposed to say or do when we meet him? I feel angry when I think of him. What if Sage Valmiki says that we have to love him and treat him with compassion, which I'm sure he will."

Kusha interrupted, "Lava, the hermitage is beautiful, and our life here is simply splendid, but at times I am so very eager to see the rest of the world. I don't want to leave Mother either, but I figure I can come by and visit her often, and once my training is complete I will stay with her forever. I don't know what our father thinks about us either. Let's just think consider that for a second! What's the worst thing that can happen? The king, our father, will probably tell beloved Valmiki that he does not want anything to do with us; that will make everyone sad, but we will still be together. Now, if he honors Valmiki and accepts us, then he must have some kindness left in him so all that we need to do is be gracious. I, too, feel anger towards our father at times, but mostly I feel sadness, especially when I see some of the other fathers here at the hermitage. And then again, I feel content with our family just as it is now. I don't want any father, or anyone else, intervening in our family. I must admit that, just like you, I too feel a bit scared and shy about meeting him."

"No, I am not!" protested Lava. "I am never scared or shy like a bride! And why do you even mention other fathers in the hermitage? I am here! I will take care of you and Mother! I will never let anyone hurt you two. I promise that – and you know that I keep my promises. Now, this is what I have decided. I will treat this father the same way he treats our mother. And I wish that you will never mention this conversation to her; she has suffered enough already and it's my job to protect her."

Lava's voice was filled with assurance and bravado. Kusha smiled affectionately at him.

It was Kusha's earth-bound thoughts and matter-of-fact explanations that had helped Lava all along, while Kusha relied on the dreams that his dear brother built for them to simply get through. There was a ray of hope – not an apparent, well-formed one but a more vague one that was like an embryo, under-developed and evolving, uncertain and fearful. It was the hope of being accepted by their father the king. Affirmations of their greatness, and the irreversibility of their destiny, were strong roots. And they could stand unshakable – if only they were accepted! Their mother – however kind, noble, loving, capable or daring – could not give them with the abiding sense of self-worth like their father provided. They hoped they would know, in whatever form it might come, that they were loved – they were indeed loved by him, their father.

At lunchtime, Sita sat beside her sons basking in the warmth of the afternoon sun, enjoying the taste of fresh fruit. Observing that the awkwardness among them had faded, she said to them casually, "Are the two of you excited about attending the great learning centers in the city of Ayodhya? You know, the very best minds from all over the empire attend these institutions. For sure, you will learn about the Vedas, which are the scriptures, but you will also be trained in all the eighteen arts including archery, hunting, and elephant lore, not to mention law, medicine, and military science. This will truly be one of the most wonderful experiences of your life."

"Will you be alright without us, Mother?" asked Lava, looking worried.

"What if the King is still angry and refuses to accept us? What if he dislikes you?" asked Kusha, in a voice filled with concern.

Sita smiled at her beautiful children, a surge of love flooding her heart, as her eyes grew moist with happiness. "What if he does dislike me? I cannot make him like me! You cannot make him like me, nor can anyone else. It will cause me pain, but I can live with that. Besides, I have the two of you who love me and I really enjoy my life here, so I will be all right."

The boys giggled as they listened to their mother, knowing and understanding. She was right, but the newness that was about to come into their life made them both a bit nervous.

Sita continued, "Now, what if he is still angry and does not accept the two of you? I cannot make him accept you. You cannot make him accept you. It will surely hurt a lot if he rejects you – and it will hurt for a long time. Perhaps the pain might even stay forever. But when you think of a thorn-filled flower bush you do not associate it with its thorns alone. do you? I wish for you to accept your life just as it is and assume responsibility for your own happiness. The learning that you will obtain at prestigious institutions is available to all capable students. It is simply the law of the land that all can be educated. And the two of you are extremely capable and bright, plus you have received a head start here at the hermitage, so I am sure you will do well there. Now, if your father does not accept you, some people might taunt you. Surely that will hurt a lot. I hope and pray that such an experience will not have a place in your lives! But if it ever does, I wish that you will experience that pain with compassion for yourself and make sure that you will be a better parent when your time comes. The only thing that we can change is our own self. And, as your mother, I ask that the two of you grow to become illustrious leaders who bear the life assigned to them with utmost graciousness and gratitude."

The boys listened attentively, their expressions filled with pride for her.

Sita continued, "All of us will always worry about each other. It is what loving families do! I will miss you both deeply and will definitely suffer the pain of being separated from the two of you. But if I hold on and refuse to let you go, we will all be miserable and unhappy. The two of you will feel unsatisfied, tethered, and resentful. And I will feel guilty for holding you back. It will become hard to love each other when we do not have room to blossom. I want the best for the two of you. I desire that both of you will grow to reach your full potential and live a fulfilled life. I am here! I will always be here for you! When you need me, you will find me in your heart always. I want you to know that I love my life and I love teaching my many students. I love enabling these people who give me so much love in return. Letting you both go will not, in any way, make me want to stop pursuing my own happiness. I am responsible for my own joy and wellbeing; you are not. I hope this helps you to make the right choices for your life."

Sita embraced them warmly. Her courage seemed to be reflected in the faces of her sons as they held her affectionately in their arms.

For a while, the three of them held the embrace until they heard a loud commotion in the distance. Curious, they turned around as one of Valmiki's disciples approached them hastily.

"Dear Sister, Valmiki, along with his entourage, is a few hours away from the hermitage. The journey has been tiring, and we have had to take many breaks to allow sage Valmiki to rest. He instructed me to ride quickly to inform Guru-Ma and you that he will soon be home. King Rama is with him, disguised as a commoner, to meet with you and his children. Please make haste and prepare to receive them. I am available for any assistance that you might need in this preparation," he added.

Sita was shocked to hear this news. A joy, the kind she had forgotten, leapt into her heart and a magnificent light came into her eyes. She raised a hand to cover the full smile that almost appeared upon her lips. In an instant, a strange fear slammed shut the doors to her heart; she stood with her face flushed, not knowing what to do.

Young Lava and Kusha received the news with nervous excitement, and they immediately turned to their mother as if seeking direction.

Guru-Ma, leaning against her stick, walked hurriedly to Sita, rescuing her from her stupor. She instructed the boys to collect firewood that would be used to heat bath water for the tired travelers. Obeying at once, Lava and Kusha disappeared.

As they ran towards the woods, Kusha held Lava's hand and said, "He came! He came for us!"

The boys exchanged a quick embrace as they rushed to perform their task.

Guru-Ma, with her arm around Sita, said, "Come my dear, let's prepare a fine meal for our honored guest! I have never even seen a King in all my life, and chances are, this will be the only King that I will ever receive in my home. We have a lot to do and much to talk about." Walking alongside Guru-Ma, Sita was too astonished to utter a single word. They were almost inside Guru-Ma's home before she said, "Guru-Ma, what am I to do? He's coming after all these years! What do I do?" she repeated.

"Nothing! You have to do nothing just yet! Let us see how things unfold, my dear. As of this moment, all we know is that weary travelers are coming into the hermitage. We do what we always do; we offer them warm water to bathe, food to satisfy their hunger, a place to rest, and we treat them with kindness. So let us do just that! Would you like some time to yourself, my child, or would you rather come along with me to my kitchen?"

"I want to be right here by you, Guru-Ma. I feel so much fear right now. What if he takes my sons away? What if he despises me? I am not prepared for any of this, Guru-Ma. Can we stop them from coming now?"

Unable to hide her panic, Sita was shaking violently.

"Hold on, my dear! Sit down! Take a few moments and breathe. Tell me what is going on," instructed Guru-Ma.

"My heart is pounding violently in my chest," Sita replied. "My belly feels nauseous, sweat is trickling down my back, my fingertips and feet are cold, I feel shivers down my spine, my teeth are chattering, my legs feel heavy, and I cannot move them! I feel fear, tremendous fear, I cannot move fast enough, and they are all leaving! They are all leaving me behind in the forest!" she screamed shrilly, tears streaming from her eyes.

Sita reached out to hold Guru-Ma and cried, then cried some more. When she finally calmed down, her heart had stopped pounding, the nauseous feeling was gone, and she had stopped shivering. She let go of Guru-Ma and exhaled loudly.

"You are safe, dear Sita!" Guru-Ma comforted her. "Valmiki found you in the forest and brought you home! You are safe here, my child! We are always here for you! Your boys – they love you more than you can ever know! Your students treasure and cherish you! You are loved deeply, and you are a loving person. You are safe here, my child."

Sita smiled as she wiped away her tears, "Yes! Yes I'm safe! I'm so sorry, Guru-Ma, my mind raced back to the day I was abandoned. One would think I would have forgotten that by now. After all these years and these many happenings."

Guru-Ma smiled. "You know there are still some mornings when I wake up afraid that Valmiki might be gone. Be kind to you, my dear. We all suffer, and we cause suffering for each other – such is the nature of our being."

As Guru-Ma spoke in her soft, gentle voice, Sita drank in her words, her strength returning to her. "Freshen up, my dear child, and get your children ready! Let us not meet the King looking like we're ready to lay down our arms and surrender."

Guru-Ma said this so lightly that Sita smiled.

✕

XX.

REUNION

Rama was quiet, as he had been all morning. His silence was weighted with the stillness that had ascended upon his heart and assumed its rightful seat upon its throne. His mind did not whirr with doubts or questions; a pristine clarity presided over him. His spirit felt light and airy, like that of a man who had faced his demons and destroyed the strong hold they once had over him. Mounted on his horse, the majestic King Rama – even in his ordinary robes – was incapable of hiding his regal demeanor.

Like a long absent traveler returning decades later to his childhood home, he too expected to see changes and to be met with surprises. Meeting the familiar once again, he was sure to have rude awakenings.

Rama trailed behind the great sage, out of reverence for his age and station, allowing Valmiki to set the pace at the end of this extraordinary journey. As they rode along the winding path, King Rama took in the scenery around him. It felt like he was walking into it, rather than observing it from the outside. Thus, the atypical greenery, the familiar blue sky, the habitual tunes of the cowherd, the tufts of grass on the paved earth, the routine of grazing cattle, the usual humming of the bees, and the practiced laughter of the brooks seemed incredibly fresh to his eyes, as if he were seeing hearing everything for the very first time.

Valmiki, on the other hand, held a leisurely conversation with his disciples, taking the time to exchange greetings with herdsmen and other wayfarers. He stopped often, sharing tidbits of history concerning the sites that they passed, explaining the medical properties of different herbs they found, inviting discussions about half-baked concepts as if it were imperative to draw well-formed conclusions. He was deliberately trying to slow the pace of this journey just to ensure that Sita and her children would have the time they needed to prepare for what was coming.

"Do you see how the path curves by the stream, King Rama?" pointed out Valmiki. "A little beyond that is where the hermitage is situated."

Catching Valmiki's glance, Rama smiled and nodded. The two men held each other's gaze for a quick moment, communicating their preparedness for what was to come.

The laughter and shouts of young boys and girls at play reached the travelling men even before they could see the hermitage. Valmiki relished the company of his young companions. Swinging down from his saddle, he stepped to the ground and stretched himself. The children came running to him. Valmiki carefully placed two young sisters on his horse and chatted as he led everyone back into the hermitage.

A little boy dressed in a loincloth – perhaps all of three years old – came running to the old sage, held his hand, and kissed it. There were more inquiries than Valmiki could possibly answer. Had he brought gifts? What was the city like? Was the King really seven feet tall with a hundred hands? Had Valmiki missed them? And on and on! Valmiki's disciples descended from their horses and led the children away from the fatigued sage, who laughed in glee like a child himself. Rama was simply amused.

Valmiki and King Rama handed their horses' reins to the disciples and slowly made their way into the hermitage. Serenity seemed to permeate the air of the hermitage, causing almost anyone who entered to exhale and let go. The peaceful environment felt lucid, comforting, and pious.

As he stepped inside, Rama could hear his own thoughts coming to his mind, effortlessly, with inescapable distinctness! He imagined the city of Ayodhya functioning at the very moment – quite remarkably, without him – and smiled as he realized his folly in assuming himself to be indispensable.

As they walked towards the humble abode of the revered sage, Valmiki took it upon himself to give Rama a brief tour. "The land in here extends from the banks of the River Tamasa to the fence all around, covering an area of about four square miles. We have fields in which we grow rice, peas, sesame seeds, wheat, barley, and cotton. Most of our fruits and vegetables are grown in this rich, fertile soil. We also receive gifts in the form of food, clothing, and cattle from the local villagers in exchange for the education we provide here."

Valmiki rested his hand on a tree trunk as he pointed toward a big banyan. When he continued, his voice was a low whisper so he would not disturb the students. "Down by the big banyan is where most of our classes are conducted. We impart learning in different fields of knowledge – the Vedas, science of yoga, basic Ayurvedic principles, reading and writing, mathematics, astronomy, martial arts, archery, music, and meditation."

Rama observed the children in their open classrooms under the sprawling banyan that looked so formidable, covering a vast area where innumerable trunks and roots were held together in its tight embrace. One section of students was sitting on the floor, busily composing poetry that they etched on parchments made of tree bark. In a different corner a few others memorized the rules of Sanskrit grammar. Further along the lengthy radius of the tree, yoga was in session, with students effortlessly assuming the mountain pose. Women and girls, Rama saw, made up a significant portion of the students who were taught here – and this was what amazed him the most.

"Dear sage," he said to Valmiki, "the great learning centers of Ayodhya feel outdated in their practice of not permitting women students. I am truly taken aback by the number of women scholars that you invite in here!"

"Yes, dear Rama, that has been a significant triumph for our hermitage! Imparting education to women has changed the quality of life here at the hermitage and in the local villages as well. In fact, some of the local village heads have gone a step further, enabling their women to participate and be more engaged in the local administration. The challenges are plenty – and there are many that remain unresolved – but by virtue of the example set by the men in the hermitage, other men in the local villages have become more tolerant and begun to accept these changes. We have ignored the wellbeing of our women for too long, dear Rama, but without our help they cannot succeed."

After a moment's pause, Valmiki said emphatically, "It is my wish, my most sincere wish, that many more men come forth to enable this transition. After all, even the most ignorant among us understands that the earth needs to be nourished in order for her to yield healthy harvests."

Rama smiled at the sage's words. He now knew of a way in which he could repay the sage for his exemplary kindness. Rama's soul felt lighter as he recognized how he could redeem himself.

"We have a few streams that pass by the hermitage and provide us with ample water," Valmiki continued. "But just last summer I had a well dug out in the far end, mostly to irrigate the soil by the mango grove situated to the north. You see, the streams are located at the southwest end, and it would be difficult to construct canals since the occupied homes are mostly in the center. The hermitage is made up of about seventy homes. We use mud bricks, wood, baked tiles, and hay for construction."

Valmiki pointed to Sita's house.

"Rama, that small hut out there, the one with a front porch, is where your family lives. Sita has done a fabulous job planting flowers in her garden – has she not?"

Rama was filled with wonder! The entire home was a third of the size of her chamber in the palace, yet it was filled with life and was beautiful. It had a thatched roof, and its mud-caked walls were covered with intricate paintings in earth colors. There were flowers planted along its outer edges and a fenced-in area to one side where Sita was raising herbs and vegetables. A small stall at the back, made out of wood and hay, was home for her cow and young calf. The ground in front of the home had been cleaned and was caked with red earth. An umber clay pot, set in front, housed the sacred tulasi herb. Surrounding it was a simple design made from white chalk powder. A lit lamp was by the doorway. This tiny dwelling did not bespeak luxury, but it exuded a great sense of warmth and deep satisfaction. All of a sudden, Rama felt a brewing impatience. He longed, with all his heart and soul, to meet his estranged wife and children.

Valmiki, reading Rama's thoughts, wished to hurry along, but his aged and fatigued body refused to pay heed. He acknowledged his own incapacity with compassion and continued walking at the pace that felt comfortable.

"Now, let us walk, down this path King Rama!" Valmiki prompted. "We are almost there! Sita, Guru-Ma and the children will all be present in my home."

So saying, he guided the King along the pathway leading to his home. Rama saw his young sons and Sita from a distance. His heart almost exploded with joy! Sita looked simply elegant! She was dressed in a sari that was the color of yellow ochre, similar to the shade of the sari that had wrapped her young body when he had first laid eyes upon her. The yellow in her sari highlighted her dark skin. Her hair, now bearing visible strands of gleaming silver, was tied back neatly into a bun. Her eyes shone with a thousand tints of the spring sun, with a luminous quality that had been preserved all these years, untouched by age or events. Her mouth bore a delicate smile that she did not try to hide. Her demeanor was calm and composed.

Now Valmiki approached Guru-Ma, greeting her warmly, eloquently praising her youthful looks and confessing how deeply he had missed her. Guru-Ma stared him down, as if urging him into quiet composure.

King Rama's steps became tentative as he walked beside Valmiki. Guru-Ma stepped forward and welcomed the king, bringing her palms together and bending her head in dignified gesture. King Rama clasped her hands within his and met her gaze with tear-moistened eyes. He whispered his deep gratitude. Even before he had risen again, he had won the heart of the old woman.

Valmiki called forth Sita and the children. The boys folded their palms and bent their head in respect to their king. Sita stood still.

With her palms folded, looking at the handsome face of King Rama, She addressed him in a soft yet clear voice: "I present to you, your sons Lava and Kusha!"

Rama looked deeply at each of them. They were beautiful, strong, graceful, filled with youthful vigor and splendor. He instinctively opened his arms, and they stepped eagerly into his embrace, as children do, feeling love for anyone loved by their mother.

"I am sorry for not being present in your lives all this time. Please forgive me my absence."

King Rama's voice was filled with equal measures of joy and sorrow as tears streamed down his cheeks. Sita's heart was overcome with tenderness and joy as she watched her sons being embraced by their father. Her own tears flowed freely, though she tried to wipe them away. Overpowered by fast-flowing emotions, she and Rama stood still as they cried.

Valmiki threw his arm around Guru-Ma's shoulders as they looked into each other's eyes and smiled.

"Are the bath waters ready for us weary travelers, my dear?" he asked.

"Yes, of course," she replied, adding with a smile, "and so is your rice pudding!"

So much time had been wasted that no one was interested in lingering very long. Just as soon as Rama bathed and emerged, looking clean and radiant, young Lava and Kusha joined their father, observing his mannerism, noting the foods that he preferred, the courtesy in his tone, the elegance in his manner, his attention to their stories. Every observation seemed tinged with enthusiasm.

After a simple yet satisfying meal composed of whole wheat bread, rice, spiced vegetables, yogurt, and rice pudding, they all moved out into the front porch. Valmiki settled down to rest after his tiring journey and soon fell asleep upon a soft pillow. Guru-Ma covered him gently with a blanket, and then excused herself on the pretext of having chores to complete. It was obvious she wanted to give the family some much-needed time of their own.

The twins continued describing everything their father wished to hear, and he raised several questions that kept them engaged and enthralled. Without a moment's hesitation, Lava accepted his father's challenge to a duel, eager to demonstrate his skill. The two of them fought with swords and wrestled, Rama giving the boy a chance to show his skill to the fullest before finally defeating him. Lava was ecstatic!

Rama quizzed his son Kusha on literature, law, philosophy, and historic battles. He was mesmerized by the knowledge that his young son possessed. The passage of time had worn out and put to sleep memories of his childhood, but now those memories seemed to turn around and come back to him like a maelstrom. Rama narrated to his children stories of his own youth and interesting times. Though time spent in happiness is sure to be followed by moments of sorrow, Rama knew that nothing could happen in the future that would wither nor wipe out the recollection of this moment lived fully with his sons.

Sita sat by them silently. Her soul felt so peaceful that it would not even stir. The anxiety of raising their sons that she had experienced over all these years had dwarfed and subsided but never left her completely. Now, in this moment as she watched Rama affectionately ruffling the neatly combed hair of Kusha while pretending to punch Lava, her anxiety dissolved. She felt as if she could close her eyes and surrender to sleep without resistance, knowing full well that Rama was now present, watching after their children. Her whole life felt complete. There was no yearning for something pending in the future – no gnawing sense that something was lack in her life, nor a longing that would plead for her attention should the doors of death open a light-filled pathway to her right that very moment. Just as she imagined herself walking towards the light, a loud voice called from behind. "Sita!" She turned, but saw no one. The father and sons were still preoccupied with play. The voice that had called upon her was her own, the soft voice residing within her soul, the one that had stuck with her through and through.

Sita wondered silently about her life. How easy it was for women to lose themselves completely in the lives of their loved ones. Forgetting, to a fault, to care for and respect one's own self, women pretended to give that which has not been received. They were like wells in a drought-ridden earth, imagining they could endlessly quench everyone's thirst.

How long had it been, she wondered, since she felt a change? How far back was the day when women forgot their sense of self? When did the moment come when, with empty breasts, they pretended to nurture young ones?

As the father and sons continued with their endless conversations, Sita gazed at Rama – his handsome profile, the floating curls of his unruly hair, his strong arms, his artistic fingers, the concentration in his eyes, his gracefulness – all of it seemed to have been preserved, remaining untouched by the passing years. Sita's heart fluttered. And just then, she caught him watching her!

"Boys, let me have a word with your patient mother." said Rama.

Abruptly, the children interrupted their chatter, suddenly realizing they had completely ignored their dedicated mother these past few hours. They were touched by guilt that a child feels when a new, favorite toy replaces an old dear one. Shyly, they walked up to their mother, hugging and kissing her more fervently than usual, as if to reassure her. Sita was simply amused.

As they prepared to walk away, Kusha whispered into her ear, "I like him!" Sita smiled and nodded her acknowledgement.

"Would you like to sit with me by the banks of the river, dear Sita?" asked Rama. "There are things I wish to share with you, and I will appreciate it greatly if you will hear me out."

There was no hesitation in Rama's voice as he held her in his gaze. Sita's felt her face flush as she experienced a warm, melting sensation within her. This was the quality in him that she had always found attractive. It was a quality, bordering on arrogant self-assurance that enabled him to simply take almost effortlessly that which he wanted.

"Sure," she replied," I will meet you there soon. I have to remind the children to light the evening lamp and complete their practice of meditation."

Rama looked at her with great endearment. He felt a pang of nervous energy within him. There was no doubt that he felt equally attracted to her, but he recognized she had changed somehow. She was no longer the blushing, self-conscious young woman he had known in the past. This Sita felt like a landscape that had emerged from the fog, now showing all its sharp colors and creases, its many roads now crisply evident. The passion of youth had made love easy and possible, burning away everything that was acquired and established like dried, dead leaves. But this would be different. While she still burnt brilliantly, she desired to burn slowly. He smiled at the foolishness of his heart, which had assumed it would simply be granted everything he wished for.

XXI.

HOME

As evening fell, the setting sun lit the sky with streaks of deep pink and purple, colors reflected in the river waters that flowed by gently, as if slowing down for slumber. The wind had gone quiet, and the spring air was filled with sweet fragrances.

Rama placed a pile of firewood near the rocks where the rivers sand was the softest; then set it alight. He wanted to make sure that Sita would be warm. He sat cross-legged on the sand, leaned back against the rocks, and gazed at the rippling waves of the smooth-flowing river.

He still loved Sita; that was for sure. But love was never the issue, was it? He had not been able to protect her, not with all the love in his heart. He wondered if there was anything left in him that was even worthwhile to offer.

From a distance, Rama saw Sita walking towards him. Her gait suggested a dreamy eloquence, one that could not be concealed nor silenced even if she had been conscious of its existence. There was a cool airiness around her. A soft melancholy marked her beautiful features; her overall appearance was one of calm composure. Rama was fascinated by the quality of her demeanor; neither confident nor shy, she seemed to occupy some territory that was unknown and exotic. She had aged gracefully. The silver strands in her hair seemed to reflect the light in her eyes, and the smile lines on her face gave her a playful expression. She had wrapped a red cotton shawl around the curves of her body and was holding it close to stay warm.

The spring air was still cool, and Sita was drawn toward the burning fire. She sat down delicately on a smooth rock, burying her cold feet in the warm river sand. A quick smile gave away a hint of nervousness.

Rama exhaled as if relieved to find her human. There was so much to be said, and yet the silence between them, the presence of each other, the flames of the warm fire, and the blue-gray twilight sky seemed to suffice in place of words. Together, now, they gazed at the disappearing horizon.

Rama sat up and looked into Sita's beautiful face, examining its splendid features.

"I am deeply sorry for my ill-thought action, dear Sita. I have caused you great suffering and pain. I ask that you please forgive me." His voice was tinged with deep sorrow, his large eyes laced with tears.

After saying these words, he instantly looked away, struggling to contain his overpowering feelings. Suddenly he felt uncomfortable. An urgent storm seemed to be carrying him unreservedly and immodestly to a place where he most certainly would be exposed. His heart felt as if it had been cast upon a fast-burning flame, and his throat quivered.

When he hesitatingly looked at Sita again, tears were flowing freely from her eyes – inviting him to share, allowing expression of the grief that each had suffered. Rama simply gave in. They cried together, silent tears streaming down their beautiful faces as if their flooded hearts had to be emptied before they could make room for words. Never before had Rama felt this vulnerable; never before had he been held so lovingly despite his vulnerability being seen by another human. His heart felt open!

The ten thousand things that each had communicated to the other since he had arrived in the late afternoon now seemed to surround them, like trees lining a plain that could only be crossed by speaking words. Words were essential. Words had to be spoken, to be heard, to convey understanding, and to express concern. After all, these words were what they had to assuage the remaining ache in their hearts and build bridges over un-navigable trenches.

Sita spoke in a soft and unassuming voice filled with concern. "What makes you think that I have not forgiven you already, dear Rama? Trust me! I am no longer angry, nor am I suffering. Please do not torture yourself with relentless criticism. I ask that you forgive yourself and move forward."

"I am extremely grateful for the loving care that you have provided our children," said Rama "I thank you for your generosity in sharing their world with me." And then curiosity made him ask, "Tell me Sita, was that a hard choice to make?"

Sita responded thoughtfully. "Guru-Ma reminds me that true love is about doing that which is right by the ones that we love, dear Rama. More than anything else, I strongly desired to secure the future of my sons. I prayed, with many prayers, that you would accept your sons; for they need to know who they are and where they come from. I thank you for your graciousness towards them. The choice that I made was difficult, but it was the result of a realization. My suffering in the hands of men made me unwilling to extend my hand in understanding. My identity as a victim was strengthened every time I came across other suffering women. I realized that, however righteous our stories, we needed the support of men to provide better endings to our own battered chapters. Ego-enhanced identity would only carry me away from my salvation! Its sole purpose was to strengthen itself – not to seek a resolution. If nature meant for a child to be borne by a mother alone, then nature would have provided for that. But such is not the case, and I realized the need for your participation. Our children would have suffered needlessly had you refused. I thank you for having the heart to grant me my wish by accepting your dear sons."

Rama was mesmerized by Sita's words. To him they felt like cool balm resting in the places within his heart that were raw from hurt. He felt drawn to her, as he had never been before.

"If I am forgiven, may I request that you come back with me to Ayodhya?" Rama asked. "I understand that it is your wish for the children to attend the great learning institutions, and I will make sure they are taught by the best of minds and the greatest of warriors. But what is to happen to us, Sita? Are we to suffer for the rest of our lives because I have erred? My life has been empty, and I have been in anguish since I banished you. I have experienced more happiness today, in this hermitage, than I ever did in the past twelve years. I do not wish to lose you once more! Please, will you consider coming back home?" Rama's voice was filled with hope.

Sita was taken back by this sudden offer. A nervous energy entered her. She found herself gazing at the smiling edges of Rama's sweet mouth, and as she looked at him it seem as if the dusk would roll over the past, diminishing it to distant forgetfulness, causing her to dance on dizzy pinnacles, throwing away what was hard-earned and stable. She closed her eyes and observed her attraction towards him with kindness. It seemed as if this attraction was expressing a desire to have him rule over her! But it slowly subsided, melting away into the corner from where it had sprung.

Sita smiled gently and spoke in a calm voice. "Surely, Rama, we have each noticed our attraction towards the other. But I hesitate to act upon such attraction alone. This choice that you ask me to make is too sudden. Much has transpired over the past twelve years, and I am no longer the woman you were once married to. Please tell, me kind Rama, why do you desire that I go back with you?"

Rama, astonished by her question, felt his heart ached as he replied, "I do not understand, dear Sita! You claim that I am forgiven, you acknowledge our mutual attraction, you desire that the future of our two wonderful children needs to be established. What, then, is the cause of your hesitation, my dear? I promise to be more considerate and thoughtful in my actions. I promise to be kind and loving. I promise to silence the voices that may dishonor you, and I truly wish to hold onto the happiness that we have experienced today. I have been alone all these years, and I have been miserable! I ask that you grace my life with your presence once again."

Noticing the anguish in his tone, Sita felt her heart open in compassion. Yet she waited a few moments before replying.

"Rama, please do not consider my questioning of your intent as refusal to concede to your wishes. Kindly forgive me this provocation. We have each pursued the other in search of happiness before; we have both failed to keep each other happy. Is this not the opportunity that has presented itself so that we can explore what we have failed at in the past?"

"Are you suggesting that my apology is not good enough and that I am incapable of keeping you happy, Sita?" Rama seemed defensive, deeply hurt by the apparent rejection.

"Kindly hear me out, dear Rama," Sita pleaded. His gaze softened as she continued. "When I first came to this hermitage I was bitter and angry because my expectations of you were unmet. I continued to suffer, for I was unwilling to take responsibility for my own happiness. Happiness, I had learned, was something that was outside of me. With the help of Guru-Ma and Valmiki, I learned the way towards my own independence, and I developed a sense of self-worth. I felt accepted with all my faults and, better yet, deeply loved despite my limitations. In here, I feel connected to the larger universe. I feel whole and complete. I do not fear that you will be unable to keep me happy, beloved Rama, I encourage you to explore, for I know that the path towards your happiness is through you and not through me."

Hearing Sita's soft tone, Rama was aware of her lack of anger and enthralled by her calm confidence. Now intrigued and desirous of learning more, he paid close attention.

Sita continued, "This enlightened sense of wholesomeness that I carry within me, it is not reserved for just a few, it is simple and within reach of all mankind. You and I are not the only ones who have suffered; in fact, there is not a single human free from suffering. Even great sages who have attained enlightenment experience suffering in the form of mild dissatisfaction from time to time. When your mind is still and your heart is free of longing, you open yourself up to a feeling of connectivity to the whole...."

As Sita struggled to find the right words, Rama recollected his experience by the river the previous night when Valmiki had decided to halt for the night. Now driven by curiosity, eager to learn, that experience came back to him. He told Sita about the feeling that had overcome him as he felt himself blending, dissolving, regenerating, and being absorbed into the fine specimens in nature.

In response, Sita's bright eyes seemed to glow with enthusiasm. She felt as if an energetic breeze had taken her up and lifted her in its arms. So he knew what it was like!

"It seems to me that for a moment in there you felt deeply connected to your surroundings," she said eagerly. "You experienced a sense of dissolution into what was around and all over. Am I correct?"

Not entirely sure where this conversation was headed, Rama acknowledged that to be true. Drawing closer, Sita went on, "You felt immense peace after that experience – did you not?"

"Yes, I felt a great stillness within me. I stopped predicting the future and allowed myself to sleep," Rama whispered, smiling openly as he observed Sita drawing closer to him.

"Now tell me, dear Rama, did that stillness feel masculine or feminine?" Sita asked.

Rama looked at her quizzically before replying in a soft voice, "Why, neither! It was simply a still clarity. I felt its presence in my body, and it filled me with peace."

Sita was clearly excited by his observation.

She exhaled deeply as a smile spread across her face. "Rama, in that moment you came as close to the divine as a human can ever come. It is called a moment of enlightenment – a sense of unity with all, and the dissolution of the self. That stillness is what can bring you lasting inner peace and happiness. I, the children, your duty towards your kingdom – we are all peripheral and transient, dear Rama. The stillness is the only thing that is permanent and peace giving. My life in the hermitage has brought me peace; my purpose here provides me with fulfillment!" she whispered.

Rama went silent for a moment. His beautiful Sita had evolved and was now enlightened. In his heart he felt great happiness and pride at her accomplishment, yet he now realized she was not ready to leave the hermitage and that brought a pang of deep sorrow. He had let her go, and now he had lost her forever – or so he supposed. "If stillness is the only truth, then why is it that we feel attraction? What is the purpose of human relationships?" he asked.

Sita smiled again. "We each suffer and we are each the cause of suffering to others. The purpose of relationships is to bring us to the presence of the stillness that exists within each of us. This is possible by observing and letting go of the fleeting thoughts, sensations and emotions that arise as a result of interaction. We will suffer even more greatly if we pursue relationships as if they could provide lasting source of happiness and joy in our lives. We, alone, are responsible for our wellbeing, dear Rama – wellbeing that can be experienced by coming back to the universal observer within each of us every time our thoughts and emotions stray."

"As far as attraction is concerned, as man and as woman we are incomplete in our external form, and we will always feel attraction towards the other. Fulfillment of our physical needs and desire does not necessarily translate into lasting fulfillment within. There will always remain an element that is so unique to a single life that it cannot be shared with another even if we want to. We can feel fulfilled and happy in a relationship and yet remain discontented as we remain unknown and unknowable in the deeper sense of our uniqueness. We cannot make the feelings of ecstatic happiness last forever. In the same manner it is possible that even though we are unfulfilled or unhappy in a relationship, we can be content and peaceful by observing the transient and being aware of the lasting presence of stillness within us. In this way a human can experience a sense of completion and inner tranquility regardless of being single or in a relationship."

"In rare instances like with my preceptors and teachers Valmiki and Guru-Ma, it is possible to enjoy both external fulfillment as man and woman, while being aware of the felt aloneness inside that can only be embraced by universal stillness and none other. In such instances we can each feel fulfilled and happy in a relationship and also continue to be comfortable with the felt aloneness within each. In such scenarios we remain aware of the transient, we remain aware of our fleeting thoughts and emotions, we can feel love and provide space for the other person as we both recognize that deep down we are all just one whole. Our life is like a drop of water in the ocean. We are both the drop of water, and the ocean. The dance of the waves upon the surface cannot alter the depth of the ocean underneath", concluded Sita.

Impressed by her understanding and yet not fully convinced, Rama asked in a soft voice filled with curiosity, "What then, my dear, is to be the purpose of human existence if we are to be free of all of our longings and fears?"

Sita nodded, replying, with a smile on her face, "I can see where the children get it from – this relentless questioning! Have faith in life and remain assured that it will bring to you all the experiences that you need to evolve. You cannot gain knowledge of the whole through intellect alone! There are a thousand different ways of learning and understanding! Sometimes you have to live the questions themselves and wait until your life is ready to receive the answers. Human life has as much purpose as humans make out of it, dear Rama. The purpose of awareness is not to discredit longings or fears but just to recognize that they are impermanent and fleeting."

"Each of us has an engaging purpose in the universe!" Sita continued. "The purpose of this river is to provide us with water and sustain the life of the creatures within it. Birds need air to fly. Infants need mothers to care. A kingdom needs a king to govern. However great or however small, all existence is valuable!"

Rama was filled with awe! "Where do I start, dear Sita? What do I do now?" His tone felt urgent, and his voice sounded determined!

"You are a king, dear Rama," Sita replied. "Your duties are towards your kingdom. This kingship is what you have pursued. Fair and impartial governance is your passionate purpose. By being aware of your thoughts, feelings, and sensations you can be more conscious of the laws that you implement within your kingdom. As for starting, you can begin right here and right now, dear Rama. Tell me – what is it like inside of you this very moment?"

"My mind is mesmerized by the knowledge I have received," he replied. "I am excited that there is a way out of this cloudiness that inhabits my mind and unhinges my sense of wellbeing. I feel an eagerness to pursue my goal towards a more conscious existence. My heart is captivated by the beauty and wisdom of this woman before whom I sit! A part of me is critical for not having recognized her inner beauty and tenderness years ago. I feel a great sense of loss as I am unable to win the heart of the woman I love!" He spoke with a taunting smile, half sad and half thrilled to be in Sita's company.

Sita sat quietly, staring at the twilight sky. The stars were resplendent – the very same stars that had shined all through these years and all through time. She smiled brightly. "You have my heart, dear Rama! You had my heart when you entered the hermitage riding behind kind Valmiki. You had my heart when you took Guru-Ma's hands within your own and whispered your gratitude. You had my heart when you embraced our sons in your arms, and you had my heart when you apologized for your errors. I only ask that you be patient. This is all much too sudden. I have worked hard and made a life for myself here, one from which I derive purpose and fulfillment. I feel great love and caring towards the people of this hermitage, and I have received great love and caring from them. Let us see what the future holds." So saying, she embraced him warmly.

Rama held her tightly in his arms and looking into her eyes he whispered, "I am sorry to cause you such anguish my dear Sita. I understand that this is all too sudden. Sage Valmiki has told me all about your work and your dedication to improving lives here at the hermitage, and I am so very proud of all of your accomplishments. We have both known just one kind of relationship between a man and a woman – the kind in which we each remained unconscious of our real selves and spent our days chasing shadows. Why not approach this differently, dear Sita? Why not we take this one step at a time and slowly? Let us wait and see how things unfold."

Sita looked at him with an expression of surprise and delight. When she nodded assent, Rama closed his eyes and smiled brightly. It felt like the universe had benevolently granted him everything that he had wished for. They sat watching the burning flames and talking with each other all night long. Just before dawn, they fell asleep in each other's arms.

People and Places

Tamasa [tamasā]: A tributary of the river Ganga, this river is known for its dark waters. The hermitage of Sage Valmiki, where this story happens is situated upon the banks of the Tamasa.

Sita [sītā]: Consort of King Rama, daughter of King Janaka and mother to Lava and Kusha, Sita is the main character of this book. Banished from the kingdom of Ayodhya by her husband and King, she is provided refuge in the hermitage of Valmiki where she undergoes the transformation to a self-realized woman.

Rama [rāma]: Consort of Sita, King of Ayodhya and son of King Dasharatha is regarded as the ideal man. In this book he is depicted as a deeply introspective human who struggles to find the balance between what is ideal and what is acceptable.

Valmiki [vālmīki]: An enlightened sage, Valmiki, is the preceptor of the hermitage situated on the banks of the Tamasa. Endorsing a lifestyle based on peaceful co-existence and compassion for all living creatures, he provides refuge to Sita when she is abandoned and imparts his knowledge and teachings to her.

Guru-Ma [guru-Mā]: A self-realized, enlightened and compassionate woman, is the consort of Valmiki and instrumental in the creation of the hermitage. With no guides or teachers, she achieves enlightenment by simply learning from her own life. The many challenges her life poses propel her towards a more aware and compassionate existence. She functions as a role-model to Sita.

Lava [lavā] and Kusha [kuśa]: Born and raised in the hermitage of sage Valmiki, the twin sons of Rama and Sita are destined for greatness. Sita their mother raises them with the hope that as future rulers they will be instrumental in establishing a society that is more kind, caring, nurturing, protective and compassionate towards women.

Lakshmana [Lakṣmaṇa]: Devoted brother of King Rama, Lakshmana, tries to dissuade him from his decision to abandon Sita in the forest. Unable to change King Rama's mind, he is ordered to take Sita and leave her in the forest.

Ayodhya [ayodhyā]: The capital of the empire ruled by King Rama.

Janaka [janakā]: Ruler of Mithila and father to princess Sita who is his only child, he gives her hand in marriage to King Rama.

Mithila [mithilā]: The capital of Sita's father, King Janaka's empire.

Ravana [rāvaṇa]: The ruler of Lanka, a devotee of Lord Shiva, Ravana, is a powerful ruler who lacks control over his passions.

Kaushalya [kauṣalyā]: The mother of King Rama, she is also the first wife of King Dasharatha.

Dasharatha [daṣarathā] – King of Ayodhya and father of Rama.

Tejas [ṭejas]: A little five-year old, who tries to distract Valmiki while he meditates, by placing a jasmine wreath upon his head.

Taru [ṭaru]: A young girl child, Taru, keeps Sita company in her early days at the hermitage.

Brugu [bṛugu]: Another enlightened sage, he is an attendee at the discourse about the origin of the universe, conducted at the hermitage of sage Valmiki.

Sanathana [sanāthanā], Govinda [goviṅda], Atreya [āṭreyā] and Lalitha [laliṭhā]: Disciples of Valmiki and attendees of the discourse about the universality and continuity of life, that takes place in the home of Valmiki and Guru-Ma.

Vedanta [veḍāṇtā], Sumana [sumanā] and Kapila [kapilā] – Disciples of Valmiki and attendees of the lesson on meditation taught by Valmiki under the big banyan.

VANDANA NITTOOR

About the Author

Born and raised in India, Vandana Nittoor has lived in the United States for almost two decades, making New Jersey her home away from home. Married, with two children, she is a "multi-tasking mom" who, in addition to her writing, is also a blogger, an artist, a gourmet chef, and an accountant by profession. A storyteller since early childhood, Vandana has continued to use writing as a tool to make sense of her world and harness her inner resources. In Banks of the Tamasa, her debut novel, the author seeks to point out a way to lasting inner peace through the timeless art of storytelling.

Made in the USA
Middletown, DE
09 August 2015